# WHAT PEOPLE ARE SAYING ABOUT THIS BOOK

"It's as if one of Stephen Ambrose's 'Citizen Soldiers' stepped out of the pages and started telling his own story. Bill McMurdie, the tall skinny kid from Pasadena, California, was a combat infantryman in some of the toughest fighting in Europe—and lived to write about it, for which we're all grateful."
— *Sigurd Lee, retired college professor of English and Drama, Bethany Lutheran College, Mankato, Minnesota*

"During these times of relative peace and prosperity, it is good for us to look back to see the dedication, sacrifice, and courage of the men and women who played a role in one of history's great moments and have thereby earned the title *The Greatest Generation.*"
— *Ronald J. Younge, VP. Academic Affairs, Bethany Lutheran College, Mankato, Minnesota*

"Bill's memoirs are not just the product of hindsight looking through the hazy window of time. They are drawn from correspondence written to parents from the field of battle. His unassuming presentation of experiences, common to his fellows, helps us to comprehend the uncommon courage of common men who fought and died for us."
— *Walt Elgin, Pastor, Honolulu, Hawaii*

"Bill McMurdie's book isn't just an accurate reminiscence, carefully documented; it is above all a 'good read,' a riveting account that I couldn't put down."

— *Rev. E. Bryant, Director of Development, Bethany Lutheran College, Mankato, Minnesota*

"A vigorous tale of war through the eyes of a teenager. McMurdie takes the reader into the dirty foxholes of WWII—through mud, cold, trench foot, dying—the basics of the foot soldier. He remembers them all. This book is a gripping view of life's fragility in war as recounted in letters home. A love for mankind forged in the crucible of war brought this young man to do God's work. Some events are so sudden, so heartless, so terrible that they shatter some people's faith, but cultivate others'. The author tells of his war."

— *Wendell R. Benson, an Iowa editor of forty years*

# Hey, Mac!

This is serious business!
A guy could get *killed*!

WILLIAM F. MCMURDIE

American Home School Publishing, LLC
Cameron, MO 64429

Copyright ©2000 William F. McMurdie
All rights reserved, including the right of reproduction in whole or in part in any form.

SECOND EDITION, FIRST PRINTING
December, 2006
American Home School Publishing, LLC
PO Box 570, Cameron, MO 64429

ISBN 0-9779000-1-0
EAN 9780977900015

Library of Congress Control Number 00-090822

Cover design by Amy McCroskey

Disclaimer: Although the author and publisher have tried to ensure accuracy and completeness of the events, they assume no responsibility for errors, inaccuracies, omissions or any inconsistencies. Events are colored by the author's viewpoint and how they affected him. Letters sent home have not been edited but have been left as written, in part or in their entirety.

## DEDICATION

This story of my experiences during World War II is dedicated especially to two men who died in battle: PFC Robert Ison, who was willing to give his life that his children and we might live in freedom, and to 1st Lieutenant Charles Gullette Jr., a true leader. He did not just layout plans and point the way but stepped out and led the way.

This story is also written in memory of my parents. Dad was a constant example of Christian faith, moral rectitude, and work rightly done. Mom guided our lives mostly by gentle persuasion and her example of courtesy and kindness and an articulate Christian faith.

"Dad"  
Lewis McMurdie

"Mom"  
Marion Jean Herbert

*(These pictures were taken shortly before my parents' marriage on September 29, 1923)*

# ACKNOWLEDGMENTS

My research for this book, and also for the reasons behind World War II, has led me to the reading of many books, including Hitler's *Mein Kampf.* The main ones I used are listed at the end of this book under Sources Consulted.

I have also had the help of many people, and I am somewhat concerned about listing any names for fear I will leave someone out. If your name is missing, I hope you realize that I appreciated your help but just could not list everyone. I list just those who gave help that I found especially and uniquely helpful.

First, my wife, Jean, since, if it had not been for her help, this book would not have been completed—especially because one day I punched something on the computer and the manuscript suddenly changed into all sentences with no paragraphs. Her help in expressing ideas in a better way was invaluable.

Rev. Michael Smith, who got my first manuscript into a form that made it possible to publish my original *Memoirs.*

Dick (Richard) Byers, one of the historians of the 99th Infantry Division, who was able to answer almost every question I had about the Division and who give me advice and counsel on a number of matters. He was able to furnish some much-needed pictures and to help with the maps. I am highly honored that he was also willing to write the Foreword.

My special thanks to all who read *Memoirs* and then wrote and encouraged my efforts—among them: Don Russell, Wendell R. Benson, Rev. Edward W. Bryant, Rev. W. Elgin, Dr. Tom Young, Ronald J. Younge, and especially Professor Sigurd Lee who gave me much support and good advice.

Taylor Publishing Company of Dallas, Texas, for permission to quote from *"DAUNTLESS"—A History of The 99th Infantry Division.*

John Bauserman, Major Stephen Rusiecki and Joe Snyder for granting me permission to quote from their books as listed under Sources Consulted.

## PREFACE

For the last few years, family and friends have urged me to record my experiences during World War II. They found out that my mother had saved almost all of my army letters and that I had written down my experiences while still in the army as a member of the occupation forces. Then too, they reminded me that the WWII GI's were dying off. "You need to write down your story." So it was that in 1999, for the first time in all these fifty some years, I sat down and read my army letters that my mother had saved, and I also read the material I had written just after the war. The result was much of what you find in this book and in an 8 1/2 x 11 spiral notebook mailed out last year to family and friends. After reading what I had written, many then urged me to put what I had written into book form.

However, to actually publish a book seemed a waste of time and effort. There are so many books. Why another? But several very good friends became insistent. The main point of their argument was that what I had written was about the life of an infantryman, in detail, and they knew of nothing quite like it. Many also remarked, "I liked what you wrote. It is a 'good read.'"

So, I decided to go ahead. To this end I consulted books about World War II and especially books about the 99th Infantry Division in which I had served in training and combat. I wanted to get my facts straight and make sure what I said was accurate. This led me into contacting the 99th Infantry Division Association. Through this association I have been able to contact men with whom I had served during the war. They helped confirm what I have written or showed me where I needed to make corrections. Their names are listed under Sources Consulted.

I also have come to realize that what I had written in the war years does contain information of historical significance. So, one reason I have written is to help fill out the historical record of World War II.

In this book, as in my former publication, I have also expressed some personal convictions about the why and wherefore of war. I do so because I think history does teach valuable lessons. I share with you the conclusions to which I was led.

I hope what I have written is not only a "good read" that pays honor to the infantryman and to the dead but that it also helps the living.

—WFM

## FOREWORD

Here is a book that tells it like it was—without heroics—without exaggeration—and, above all, without complaining about the injustice of being snatched from a relatively comfortable, army-sponsored, engineering education and being thrust into the miserable life of a front-line combat infantryman; thus into the biggest battle ever fought by the U. S. Army during any war and during the worst European winter in fifty years.

It is hard to imagine the misery and privation suffered by these men in the front lines, but without them and their dogged perseverance at the nastiest job in the world, we would all be leading a far different life today.

Wm. McMurdie does an admirable job of telling what it was like to live in constant danger and almost unendurable wet and cold and yet to survive with his honor, integrity and modesty intact.

Today everyone who served in the armed forces is called a "hero," but this is the story of the true heroes, the combat infantrymen, by one who was among them.

—*Richard H. Byers, "C" Battery, 371st Field Artillery, 99th Infantry Division*

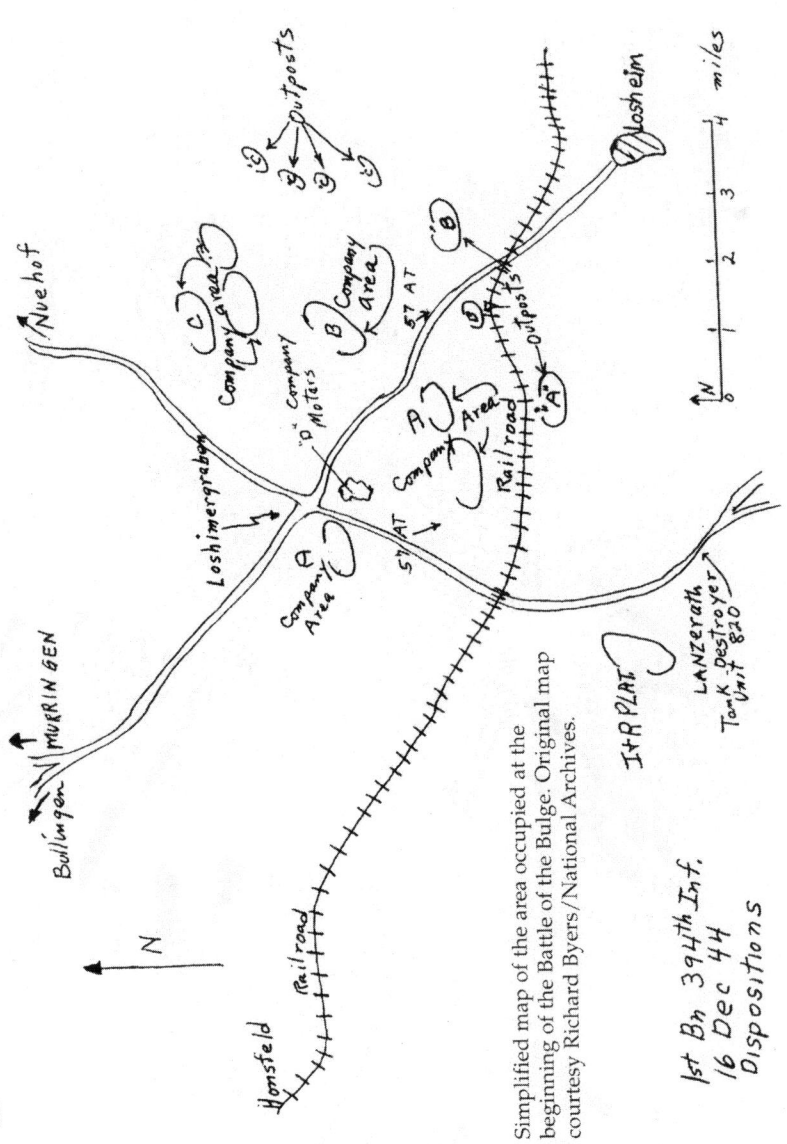

Simplified map of the area occupied at the beginning of the Battle of the Bulge. Original map courtesy Richard Byers/National Archives.

MAP 1

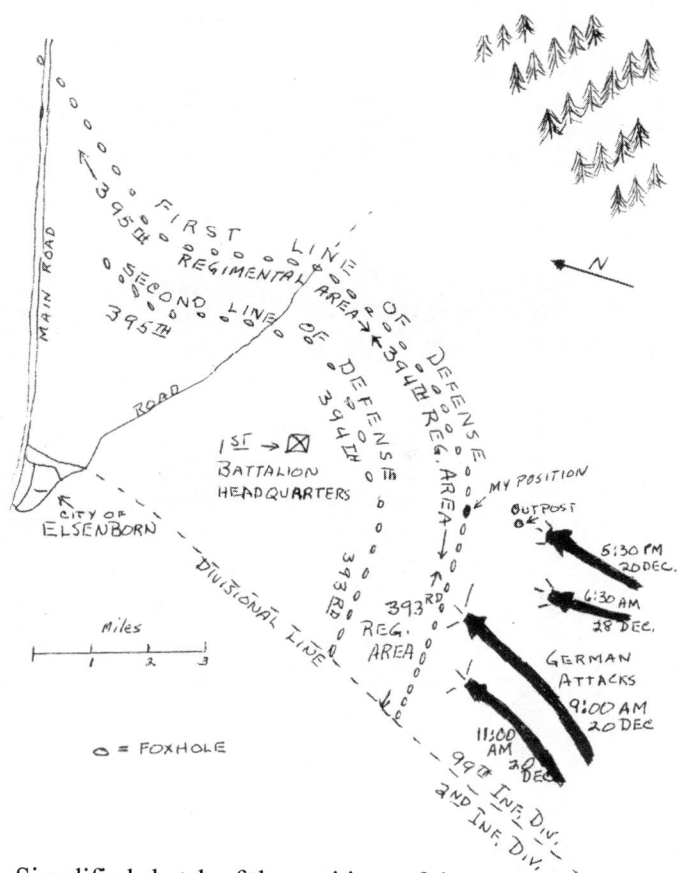

Simplified sketch of the positions of the 393rd, 394th, and 395th Infantry Regiments of the 99th Infantry Division from December 19, 1944 to February 1, 1945. The Elsenborn Ridge, where we were dug in, was called the HOT CORNER because the Germans hurled three heavy attacks on the area December 20th. Only the one at 5:30 p.m. hit our area; the other two were to our right. We were also hit again on the 28th. Note the woods from which we took the prisoners and the the 1st Battalion Headquarters and Command Post.

MAP 2

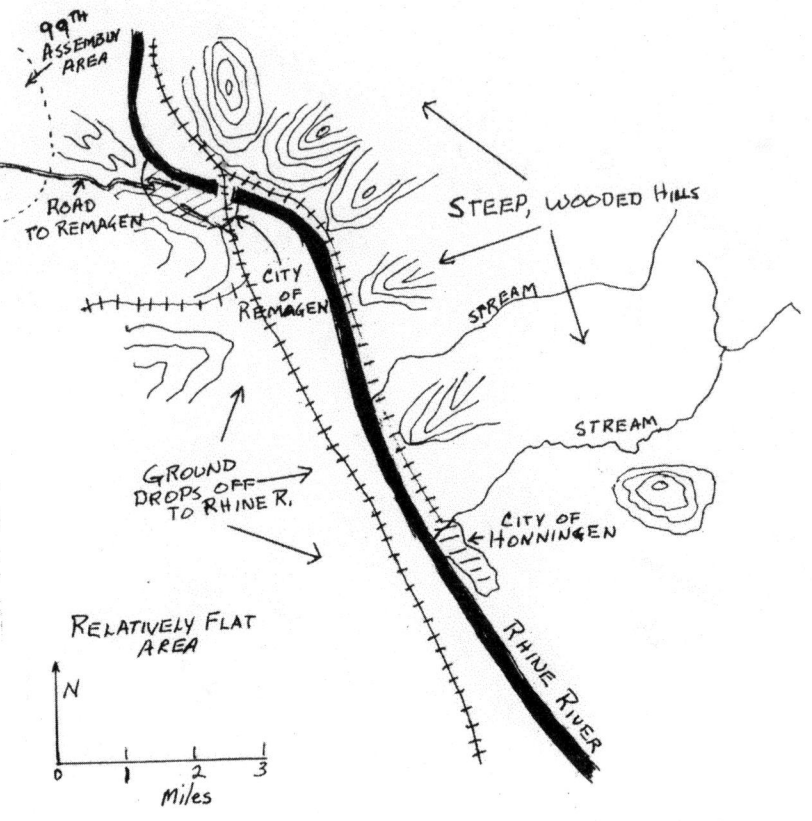

Simplified map of the Ludendorf Bridge-Remagen Bridgehead where we fought begining March 9, 1944. Note the city of Honnigen and the stream going through it to the Rhine. This map is a simplified form of the map on page 221 in "DAUNTLESS."

MAP 3

# CONTENTS

Dedication .................................................................. vii

Acknowledgments ....................................................... ix

Preface ....................................................................... xi

Foreword .................................................................. xiii

Map One .................................................................. xiv

Map Two ................................................................... xv

Map Three ................................................................ xvi

Taking the First Step ................................................. 19

Camp Chaffee, Arkansas ........................................... 23

Jonesboro, Arkansas ................................................. 30

Fayetteville, Arkansas ............................................... 30

Camp Maxey, Texas .................................................. 37

Trip to Camp Myles Standish, Massachusetts ........... 57

Camp Myles Standish ................................................ 57

Trip to England .......................................................... 58

Bridgeport, England .................................................. 61

Into Battle ................................................................. 66

Battle of the Bulge .................................................... 83

On the Attack to the Rhine ...................................... 127

Remagen Bridgehead .............................................. 140

Paris, France ........................................................... 164

Hospital in England ........................................................ 166
Back to the 99th Division ............................................. 174
Marktheidenfeld, Germany ........................................... 180
Neuendettelsau, Germany ............................................. 185
MP-Furth, Germany ...................................................... 189
Marktheidenfeld am Main ............................................ 199
Dachau ............................................................................ 199
Munich, Germany .......................................................... 207
Malmedy Massacre ........................................................ 209
Homeward Bound .......................................................... 215
Wunsiedel, Germany ..................................................... 217
Bremerhaven, Germany ................................................. 219
At Sea ............................................................................. 220

Epilogue ......................................................................... 225
Honor Roll ..................................................................... 230
Sources Consulted ......................................................... 232
Appendix 1 .................................................................... 235
Appendix 2 .................................................................... 236
Photos ............................................................................ 237

## TAKING THE FIRST STEP

The lights went out and a siren sounded. Plunged into darkness, I wondered just what was happening. Whatever was happening, it was new to me.

I had turned eighteen on January 8, 1943. On April 6th I received the following:

> **ORDER TO REPORT FOR INDUCTION**
> **The President of the United States, Franklin Delano Roosevelt**
> **To: WILLIAM FRANCIS MCMURDIE**
> **Order No. 12,307**
>
> GREETING:
>
> Having submitted yourself to a local board composed of your neighbors for the purpose of determining your availability for training and service in the armed forces of the United States, you are hereby notified that you have been selected for training and service in the ARMY.
>
> You will, therefore, report to the local board named above at PACIFIC ELECTRIC WAITING ROOM, FAIR OAKS AVE. 7 UNION ST., PASADENA at 7:15 a.m. on the 17th day of April, 1943.
>
> The local board will furnish transportation to an induction station of the service fo which you have been selected. You will there be examined, and, is accepted for training and service, you will then be inducted into the stated branch of the service. Persons reporting to the induction station in some instances may be rejected for physical or other reasins. (Etc.)

Notice the last line, "may be rejected for physical or other reasons." So the first step in entering the Army was a physical examination. And I'll never forget that examination. We had barely filled out a few forms, and taken some kind of test, when we were asked (commanded?) to take off all of our clothes. And I mean ALL. Then we got in line and went from one doctor to another, where each examined us for one thing or another. This examination included punching and prodding us here and there to find out what, I don't know. All I can remember is that even though I was used to the high school locker room and taking showers with the masses at Pasadena Junior College, I felt this was about as dehumanizing an experience as I had ever gone through.

At least I did not have the experience of one fellow serviceman I have read about recently. He wanted to get in but was underweight. He therefore ate a lot of bananas and drank a lot of milk before reporting for the physical. He now weighed enough, so continued in his examination. But, he suddenly had to throw up, and up came banana after banana. When that problem ended, he came to where he had to give a urine specimen. He was given a test tube from a rack of 24 and told to produce. He did, but once he started he could not stop. He ended up filling up all 24 test tubes. He then took the whole rack of tubes to the technician. He records how the technician took the rack of test tubes and looked at them, and then looked back at him, and then back at the filled test tubes, and then again at him, with an expression of utter awe.

I believe we went home after our physicals. We were told to report one week later at the same place. So, on April 24th, the first day of Easter vacation, and in the middle of the second semester of the school year, World

War II began a whole new life for me. My father drove me to the Old Red Car Electric Streetcar barn on Fair Oaks Street in Pasadena, California. I got aboard the car at the crack of dawn, and the old RED CAR went into Los Angeles. Almost immediately we were put on trucks and taken to Fort MacArthur, arriving there at 10:30 a.m. to be greeted by the fellows already there with the greeting, "You'll be sorry!" By 2:30 p.m. I had given up all my clothing and been given a complete uniform. At 3:00 p.m. I received two shots in the left arm, and by the next day (Easter Sunday) was not feeling too well. In spite of this, I was on KP (Kitchen Police), which simply means you do whatever the cooks tell you to do.

The next day we began taking written tests that were to be used to assign us to a proper place in the Army. We were also given more shots, which left me feeling sicker. If they had nothing else for us to do, we were given the job of policing the grounds. This meant going around picking up cigarette butts or any other piece of trash. Whites and blacks were still together. Then one day they separated us. They explained that we were going to different outfits.

It was that night, as we were preparing to get to bed, that the siren sounded with an ear-shattering noise, and the barracks lights went off. Was it a drill or what? We heard the sound of the door of the barracks opening and saw the muted glow of a flashlight moving toward us. A voice yelled out, "Men, a Japanese submarine has been reported off the coast and we are a prime target. Form a single file and follow me into the trenches." We dutifully went out the barracks door and then walked between the barracks and up the hillside that forms part of the Palos Verdes Hills. Into the trenches we went, stumbling over one another in the pitch blackness of the night. Suddenly there was the sound of an artillery piece being fired. The sound came from the area of the barracks which we had just left. I suddenly felt that we were perhaps really going to be shelled by a Japanese sub. We began to talk among ourselves but were told to "shut up." We shut up. Perhaps half an hour went by before we were marched back into the barracks and were told that it was all a false alarm. All these events took place in almost total darkness, since blackout conditions were being maintained. We were told to hit the sack because we had a lot to do the next day.

The next day as we walked to the mess hall we saw a very large artillery piece with half a "barracks" behind it and the other half in front of it. I had to admit that this was good camouflage since I had thought it was just another army barracks like the one we were in. An officer informed us that the shell casing from the gun that we had heard being fired had ejected and badly smashed a part of a nearby barracks.

Each of the barracks was two-story. Entering, you went down a hall which had showers on one side and wash basins and a latrine on the other. Then there was a large open room, perhaps 50 feet long and 20 feet wide, with 10 two-deck bunks on one side of the room and 10 on the other. Upstairs there were several small rooms for the sergeants, while the rest was a large room exactly like the one below.

I was at Fort MacArthur about 10 days. After this, along with a number of others, I was assigned to the 14th Armored Division that was just then being formed at Camp

Chaffee, Arkansas. We were taken by truck to the railroad station in Los Angeles. I had to walk from the truck to the train with a barracks bag full of equipment. It was so heavy I did not think I was going to make it. A small bag of personal things I was also carrying became less important the farther I walked. But I made it to my seat on the train without dropping anything. Our destination was Fort Smith, Arkansas, the major city near Camp Chaffee. I saw Mom and Dad and Jean and Jack (my sister and brother) at the Union Station. It was sure good to see them after a week or so of being away. But, I could not say I was homesick. Things were so new and interesting and things were happening so fast that I did not have time to feel home sick. And so, off we went. We were in Pullman cars, so it was fairly comfortable. But, the trains were not air-conditioned, so when we opened the windows to get a little fresh air, coal smoke and soot blew in. For entertainment on our trip we played cards. When the train stopped, we got off and looked at whatever was around.

As we traveled across country, I mailed postal cards home which show that we traveled through Tucson and Douglas, Arizona; then through El Paso, Fort Worth and Dallas, Texas; and then on to Fort Smith, Arkansas. In a letter dated May 3, 1943, written from just outside Fort Worth, I wrote, **"Yesterday it was 98°..."**

## CAMP CHAFFEE, ARKANSAS
### MAY 4-AUGUST 5, 1943

At Fort Smith, Arkansas, we had to go through the barracks bag ordeal again. It is surprising how heavy they are, how hard it is to get them up on your shoulder, and then walk with them. We finally got on buses that took us to Camp Chaffee.

Immediately upon arrival, the Commander of the 3rd Armored Group gave us a speech. He had an eagle on his shoulder, and someone said he was a colonel. His speech, in brief, was, "Men, you're preparing for combat, so do your duty, do it right, and do it the way you are told." At home the following notice appeared in the local Pasadena, California, newspaper on May 14, 1943:

### William F. McMurdie Now at Camp Chaffee

Pvt. William F. McMurdie, son of Mr. and Mrs. Lewis McMurdie, 1954 Brigden Road, Pasadena, has reached Camp Chaffee, Ark., where he has been assigned to the headquarters company of the 3rd Armored Group. Before he joined the Army last April 17, Private McMurdie was a student at Pasadena Junior College.

Basic training in the armored force consisted of learning military courtesy and discipline, vehicles and how to operate them, airplanes and how to identify them, compasses and how to read them, rifles and other guns and how to fire them. It was just one class after another, plus drill, drill, and more drill. In the evenings we usually went to the PX (Post Exchange—a grocery store with added features.)

On May 27, 1943, I wrote a letter home:

Dear Grandma and Gramp,
"**This weather out here really is terrible. It rained this morning, and now the sun is shining and it is hot and muggy.... We can't chew gum in class or ranks**

(my grandmother loved to chew gum), **so I don't chew it. And I don't smoke either** (my grandfather smoked). **. . . They told me yesterday that they plan to make a radio man out of me. I hope they do. School on radio starts Monday and I am to attend. Good-bye for a while, Bill"**

Discipline was maintained by making an unruly solider "run the gauntlet." Just seeing this form of punishment carried out once convinced me it was best I do my duty. If you are unfamiliar with this punishment, it consists of this: two rows of from 20 to 30 men face one another at a distance of about 8 feet. Each man takes his belt off and holds it at the buckle end. The unruly soldier must now run between the two rows of men, while each man in the row must try to hit the running soldier with his belt. The unruly soldier rarely runs the gauntlet without being hit several times very soundly, and often ends up in tears of pain.

Once in a while we took trips in our vehicles. Our training company had half-tracks. We would go into the countryside for different training exercises. Arkansas seemed a very wild country compared to what I was used to in California. The trees grew thick and green, as did everything else. The ground was a reddish brown, and with many vehicles crossing certain areas, the reddish dust was everywhere. We learned to drive in convoy; and, at night to move under blackout conditions. Food and water were brought to us in jeeps. During this time I am sure I wrote home to my parents, but for some reason I do not have complete letters written from Fort Chaffee, Arkansas. I have found excerpts from some of them. One dated May 31, 1943, says:

"A Sergeant Levine, who is 30 years old, is my Sgt. ... I think he likes me because I don't say anything against him being Jewish. Some fellows make a joke of it. Others are more careful."

Then on July 1, 1943:

"Sgt. Levine was busted the other day on the range. He is now a buck private. The Captain called him all kinds of names and the Sgt. said he didn't like it, right to the Captain's face. The Captain got mad and told him to come and see him later."

When not in camp, we slept in our shelter half or "Pup" tents. Two men, each with a half of the tent, would work at buttoning the two halves together and then with two short tent poles, tent pegs and rope, put up the tent. They were very small, just large enough to crawl into and lie down and sleep. I found the ground very hard. But the mosquitoes and chiggers were the biggest problem. They seemed to be everywhere. We kept all our clothes on for protection from the bugs. Even then they got to you. I don't know which was worse, the mosquito bites or the chiggers getting under your skin. Both led us to scratching ourselves. But we soon found that there was a way to shorten the time the chigger bites would bother us. We would light up a cigarette, get the end white hot, and then put the lit end as close to the bite as we could bear. The chigger would come out, and the itching would not be so bad or last so long.

*Shelter half or "Pup" tent. (From "DAUNTLESS", by permission of Taylor Publishing Co.)*

Usually, however, we got to spend the evenings in the barracks. The most lasting memory of those days is that of one very homesick fellow from Texas. Almost every night he would sit on the stairs at the back of the barracks, strum his guitar, and sing especially one song:

*YOU ARE MY SUNSHINE*

*The other night, dear, as I lay sleeping,*
*I dreamed I held you in my arms,*
*When I awoke, dear, I was mistaken,*
*So I hung my head and cried—*

*You are my sunshine, my only sunshine,*
*You make me happy—when skies are gray.*
*You'll never know, dear, how much I love you—*
*Please don't take my sunshine away.*

*You told me once, dear, you really loved me,*

> *And no one else could come between.*
> *But now you left me and love another,*
> *You have shattered all my dreams.*

I must confess that I had no sympathy for the fellow at the time. Now I wish that I had talked to him. Perhaps he did have a girl who had deserted him for someone else, was very homesick, and needed a little comfort from a friend.

Of course it rained. On a one-week "problem" (a name for practicing a certain type of warfare), we discovered what is meant by an intermittent stream bed. We had put up our tent in a nice comfortable spot, but without looking at the terrain. It rained and soon we found we were camped in a stream bed. We got soaked and so did some of our equipment. When I got up to stand guard, it was really a miserable situation. But slowly you do dry out under your rain slicker.

Guard duty was a big part of army life, along with KP where you had to not only serve food to the troops but also wash and put away what seemed like 1000 forks, spoons, and knives along with plates and cups. And worst of all was cleaning up the big pans the cooks used to prepare all the food.

In basic training I was learning much I had never known before. After a week out on the field, learning about booby traps and mines, reading a compass, setting up camp, and digging latrines, etc., we got back to camp. We suffered no colds or casualties, but when we came into camp, we were all feeling tired. The first thing we did was take a shower. I thought that at last my skin had turned a nice even brown color, but soap and water soon showed that I was still freckled.

"Hey, Mac, lend me $25." The fellow in the bed right across from me was speaking. He was a tall fellow, and very well built, massive in his shoulders and upper body, and slim at the waist. I remember his name, but will not give it, for reasons you perhaps can guess as I tell the rest of this part of my story. As I looked at him, I did so with fear. He was not only a big man but had an air about him that was very intimidating. I did not really want to lend him any money but was afraid to say no, so I said, "Sure, as long as you promise to pay me back on payday." "Oh, sure, I'll pay you back on payday. No problem," he said. Well, payday came. But he made no move at paying me what he owed. So finally I said to him, "Hey, how about the money you owe me." His answer, said with a peculiar grin on his face that frightened me a little, "What money?" I just looked at him for a second or so and walked away. His looks sent the message, "I just dare you to call me a liar." In time I talked with other fellows about my experience. Their response was, "Oh, you too?" Then one day I came into the barracks and all of this man's stuff was gone and his bunk was empty. "What happened to——?" I asked. The sergeant answered, "Oh, he is in jail." Well, I have to admit that I was half glad to hear that. It was the first time that I had had to deal with an out and out thief, and it had been a frightening experience.

## JONESBORO, ARKANSAS
## AUGUST 6—AUGUST 15, 1943

On August 3, 1943, I was told to pack up. It seemed that the Army had decided to send me to ASTP (Army Specialized Training Program). I said good-bye to some friends and then left camp to catch a bus in Fort Smith. The bus took me by way of Little Rock, Arkansas, to Jonesboro, Arkansas. For the first time I experienced something I had never experienced before. The Negroes (that is how we spoke of blacks then) were restricted to the back of the bus. In Pasadena we had people of all colors and races at school. I still remember Tommy Knot (Black) and Mitsu Matsumoto (Japanese). But perhaps I remember them so well because I, too, stood out as "different," since I was red-headed and freckle-faced.

## FAYETTEVILLE, ARKANSAS
## AUGUST 16, 1943—MARCH 9, 1944

We stayed a week at Jonesboro and were processed and assigned to a college. And so it was that I arrived in Fayetteville, the city where the University of Arkansas is located. The people there were very nice to us, and though they didn't really seem to love our presence, they tried to make us feel at home. And by "we" I don't mean just the group of us from the Army but another group from the Air Force.

My classes were not too hard, and the life was much the same as any college student. The big difference was that we had to march between classes. The Air Force fellows also had to do the same. We each tried to outdo the other in marching "correctly." We would also sing as we marched and try to out-sing the Air Force men. Two of our favorites were *Pistol Packin' Mama* and *Onward Christian Soldiers*. One of the fellows would sing a verse of *Pistol Packin' Mama* and then we would come in on the chorus:

> *Lay that pistol down, Babe, lay that pistol down, Pistol packin' mama, lay that pistol down.*

We would all sing *Onward Christian Soldiers,* but as I remember, we only sang the first verse:

> *Onward Christian soldiers, marching as to war, with the cross of Jesus, going on before.*
> *Christ the royal Master leads against the Foe; forward into battle, see His banners go!*
> *Onward Christian soldiers, marching as to war, with the cross of Jesus going on before.*

Our singing and other things must have gotten out of hand.

My December 31, 1943, letter records:

Dear Mom and Dad,
**"New regulations have come down for this semester. All men will sleep on post. Corporal punishment or KP can be handed out. Reveille every day, no days off, extra classes on Saturday. No more singing—we express ourselves too well, and are to march at rigid**

*32 William F. McMurdie*

attention. There has been almost a riot over these orders. Guys are trying to get them changed. . . . Everyone is refusing to study. Now they won't let the fellows flunk out."

All in all I rather enjoyed my time in ASTP. Also, for the first time in my life in the Army, I met someone that I really thought I wanted to get to know better. He was Clark Cavett. We called him "Happy" because that was the way he always seemed to be, and he also was always doing all he could to make others happy. He did this by showing an interest in you, who you were and what you thought. When fellows got sick, he would stay up with them at night and try to help them. A fellow thinks a lot of someone that will do that. I was surprised one day to have him tell me that he hoped to be a preacher one day.

L/R Front: CLARK (Happy) CAVETT, Arsenalt, Brajkovitch. Middle: Baughman. Back: Chesboro, Ambellows, Bailey, Burdette.)

After classes and supper the section (20 men) would have to go to study hall. Besides studying, we argued over many problems. One of our favorite subjects seemed to be the blacks and the whites. Some Southerners were very open in saying they felt they had a problem in the South and needed to solve it. But others maintained that the Negro was okay as long as he was in his place, and that that place was far away from any cordial relations with any whites. No, they didn't consider them inferior people, but "the blacks sure had better watch their step."

(Appendix 1 has the names of all of the men in our Section O-1.)

In December we all got a little vacation, and I used it to visit with the Fecht family in St. Louis, Missouri. These were relatives of my best friend, Art Ude. Art and I knew one another mainly because both of our families attended Mount Olive Lutheran Church in Pasadena, California. We also had been attending Pasadena Junior College together at the time I was drafted. A postal card dated December 27, 1943, says:

**"Had a swell time with the Fecht family and Mrs Ude. I spent two whole days and one night in St. Louis. I think I had about the best time I ever had outside of home even if Art wasn't here."**

A postal card in February lists grades, and thus shows what we studied: History-B, Geography-B, English-C, Military-B, Chemistry-A, Physics-A, Analytics-A. On the same card I notice the address is Co. A, ASTU #3875; Section O-1; U of A, Fayetteville, Arkansas.

In February we heard that the government decided to rethink the ASTP program. Some felt that it was a luxury that our nation could not afford. Men were needed to fight the war. So we were put aboard a train and shipped to Camp Maxey, Texas, and the 99th Infantry Division.

Major Stephen M. Rusiecki in his 1996 book, *The Key to the Bulge: The Battle for Losheimergraben,* says this about what happened: "The 99th Division, commanded by the capable MG (Major General) Walter Lauer, was one of these 'green' units that needed frontline experience. . . . The average soldier in the ranks was of extraordinarily high quality. Many came from the Army Specialized Training Program (ASTP), which trained and educated men with a high academic aptitude. The young recruits chosen for the program would attend some form of civilian education, such as college, and then proceed to Officer Candidate School (OCS). However, because of the immense manpower shortage caused by the reality of war, the program failed. These young ASTP men became replacements in the combat units fighting overseas, most going as basic infantrymen." (pp. 7-8)

As we entered the gates of Camp Maxey, our hearts fell. We saw that the 99th was an Infantry Division, and none of us really wanted to be infantrymen. I decided to make the best of it, as did Happy. We both agreed that the Lord knows best. This was also the advice that I received from my parents after telling them where I was. It was at this time they began saving all my letters. I am not sure why they saved them. Was it because they thought that I might not survive and wanted something to remember me by? Or did I ask them to please save them? I really do not know. For sure, I was beginning to wonder more and more what this war was all about. I was also beginning to experience the truth of what Dick Beyers, one of the main historians of our 99th Infantry Division said to me just a few days ago, "We all fought our own war." How true. We each fought for our very lives, but not just against an enemy. We also fought against the weather, against friendly fire from our own troops, and against circumstances beyond our control. How we came out of the battle was really not just up to us, but surely mainly the mercy and grace of God. And part of my struggle was trying to make "sense" of WWII itself.

After much study over the years I believe one reason behind WWII was revenge. Many take this position. All agree that during WWI Hitler had been a good soldier. Toward the end of the war he was gassed, and when the war ended was in a hospital. In time he heard of the agreements made to end the war. He considered them very hateful and unjust. So did most Germans. Charles B. Flood in *Hitler, the Path to Power,* points out that a German diplomat wrote to President Wilson pleading for justice for Germany:

"Today we stand on the verge of annihilation; a fate which cannot be avoided if Germany is to be crippled as those who hate us wish."

Then Mr. Flood points out that President Wilson's efforts to obtain justice for Germany were turned aside "in the face of Clemenceau's desire for revenge." (pp. 250, 251). (Clemenceau was the leader of France.) The *Reader's Digest's* "Illustrated Story of World War II" (p. 84), records a war correspondent's (Wm. Shirer) witness to Hitler's actions after the conquest of France, and at the signing of France's surrender. Hitler reads the inscription on a monument ending World War I:

"Here on the eleventh of November 1918 succumbed the criminal pride of the German Empire—vanquished by the free people it had tried to enslave."

Shirer then says, "Hitler steps off the monument and contrives to make even this gesture a masterpiece of contempt. He glances back at it, contemptuous, angry—anger, you almost feel, because he cannot wipe out the awful, provoking lettering with one sweep. . . . He glances slowly around the clearing, and now, as his eyes meet yours, you grasp the depth of his hatred. But there is triumph there, too—revengeful, triumphant hate."

In his book about the fall of France in 1940, Shirer writes about the same incident, "The German party, which included Goering, General Brauchitsch, Grand Admiral Raeder and Rudolph Hess, then climbed into the WAGON-LIT followed by the dejected members of the French delegation. General Keitel . . . opened the proceedings by reading a declaration which could only have been written by Hitler - so full of his customary historical distortions, his blinding hatred of the French, his passion for revenge. Going back to the terrible *wrongs* done the Germans by the Allies in 1918 (as Hitler did in dozens of speeches I had to listen to during my stay in Nazi Germany), blaming France and Britain for having started the present war. . ." *(The Collapse of the Third Republic,* by William L. Shirer, p. 879). Notice the words "going back to the terrible *wrongs."* In his speeches Hitler referred to the way the Germans were treated at the end of WWI. This shows that the German people felt as Hitler did.

To me it shows the truth of what the Bible teaches, "What you sow you reap." England and France were the two great world powers at the end of WWI. Most historians agree that they dictated a very hateful, unjust agreement ending WWI, thus sowing the seed for the events leading to WWII. So I believe one reason some of us fought in WWII was because we were reaping what England and France had sown—hate and revenge. Our treatment of Germany, Japan, and Italy after WWII was surely much better.

## CAMP MAXEY, TEXAS
## MARCH 9-SEPTEMBER 12, 1944

Camp Maxey brought more basic training, but this time infantry training. We got up at 6:30 a.m., worked hard learning to march, to take down an M-1 rifle, clean it, and put it back together again, even in the dark. We were put on all kinds of details, and went to bed about 11:00 p.m. mighty tired. Happy was sent to A Company of the 393rd Infantry Regiment, while I went into A Company of the 394th. This meant that many of the men making up the 99th were from ASTP. The only ones I knew from before were Borkowski and Prentiss. My training squad was made up of Staff Sergeant Davies as squad leader, myself, Mings, Haefner, Ison, Scartz, Ketron, Senft, Paegler, Seagraves, and Corporal Boyles, assistant squad leader. (I am missing one man but can't remember whom.) We worked hard together and we all thought that we had a good squad. Quotes from letters I sent home give an idea of our training, and our thinking during this period.

March 12: Dear Mom and Dad,
"Yesterday, Major General Walter Lauer gave us a talk and welcomed the 3,000 ASTP into the Infantry. (15,000 men made up a division.) Others of the brass spoke. A First Lieutenant told us that the Infantry was the queen of battle, etc., etc. He made the Infantry sound glorious, told us a lot of baloney, and treated us like a bunch of high school boys. I am afraid he failed miserably in his speech to improve our morale."

Major General Walter Lauer was the CG (Commanding General) of the 99th Infantry Division, and would remain so until the 99th was deactivated in September of 1945. In his book, *BATTLE BABIES: The Story of the 99th Infantry Division in World War II,* he writes of the Division receiving "more than 3000 men released from the Army Specialized Training Program, the ASTP. They took the places of the men who were released by the 99th Division during maneuvers to go to the 85th and 88th Infantry Divisions, scheduled for early departure overseas. The ASTP men were a welcome asset." (Lauer, p.99)

March 14: Dear Mom and Dad,
"I have just finished cleaning my M-1 rifle. I took the thing completely apart. Every piece until all I had was the stock, barrel (one long hunk of metal with a hole in it) and a whole lot of little pieces. I know their names, but I don't think it would help if I told them to you. . . . We are being assigned to this Company, so I suppose I will be in the Infantry. The Infantry has priority over every other branch which

means it will be impossible to get out of it. I don't particularly care - except not learning anything practical. There is a war on and it seems to need winning."

While at Camp Maxey, we noticed German POWs (Prisoners of War). So in a letter:

March 15: Dear Mom and Dad,
"I am in the eye clinic at Camp Maxey. . . . Sitting right across from me about 10 feet away are 5 German Prisoners. One of our boys named Mac Lean is talking to one of them - against the rules. Another one just walked in. There are (another came in with hob nails on his shoes) about 3 guards. They are part of Rommel's Africa Corps. One of them is quite young - all of them look like any of the rest of us. . . . All of them seem to be somewhat awe stricken at the sight of the Negro soldiers."

March 24: Dear Mom and Dad,
"We awoke today to a clear ice cold morning. . . . We had a nice G. I. Party, and washed up the barracks last night. It really looks nice now. Maybe you would like to know what we do. Well, half the men take the windows, the other half the floor. Well, we got the floor. First the beds on one side are all put into the center of the room. Then I put soapy water on the floor (which is wood), scrubbed floor with brooms, sweep that away, put clear hot water on, sweep that off, then mop up what's left. Then put beds back and repeat down other side, then down the center. . . ."

March 28: Dear Mom and Dad,
"Some of the boys were at the hospital again today. The POWs (German prisoners) were waiting on the tables. One of the boys says he was worked on (teeth) by a German doctor who had a German waiting on him. Said he did good work, too. . . . I don't seem to be getting any bigger. I still weigh 170 lbs. I wish I could get a little chubbier. We get up at 6 a.m., lights out at 9:00 p.m. . . . Our lunch was composed of stew (darn good too), macaroni, sweet potatoes, salad, bread and butter, grape fruit juice and cookies. The meals sure have improved. — Well, we got back from Dallas at 8:30 p.m. Sunday. We stayed in Dallas from 9:30 p.m. Saturday night till 5 Sunday afternoon."

April 6: Dear Mom and Dad,
"They have been working us from 5 a.m. in the morning until 10 p.m. at night since Sunday. I really haven't had a chance to do much on my own. We have finished shooting yesterday. I got 181, which is expert at most camps. We have been getting up at 5 a.m., getting to the range at 7 and starting to shoot at 8, finishing at 6 p.m. After that we have to come back and eat, clean up. It takes quite a time. We have been getting about 7 hours of sleep or less. I am in the pits pulling targets with the rest of the company. . . . Well, I still must clean my rifle M-l, caliber 30, air cooled, gas operated, clip fed. It has to be clean or I'll get a little extra detail."

April 12: Dear Mom and Dad,
"Today we went through the infiltration course. They had six 30 caliber machine guns shooting over our heads. It wasn't very hard, but crawling 75 yards is

*Infiltration Course*

enough to kill a guy. I could hardly run after I got through. One guy passed out. It must be tough on some of them. My rife was full of dirt, my rifle belt got lose and was dragging out behind me, I broke my watch chain, got my pack caught in the barbed wire, and generally messed up. I learned a lot — don't carry valuables, have equipment secured securely and go through the barbed wire face up. The bullets went right over. I could see them (tracers) go about a foot over Prentiss head.... The rest of the day we had aerial photography, reading and distance estimation and a parade. The aerial photography is fun, the distance estimation tough...."

April 13: Dear Mom and Dad,
"... Today we ran the grenade course. Throw them at trenches, holes, windows. Tomorrow we go on the close combat course. Shoot at targets when they jump up in front of us."

April 16: Dear Mom and Dad,
"... I went to church this morning. It is the first good service I have been to in the Army. ... The sermon was about Christ being the same yesterday, today, and tomorrow. It was very good, sounded awfully Lutheran, especially his German accent."

April 17: Dear Mom and Dad,
"... Well, I finally have decided to put down my opinion of bolt action rifle against semi-automatic rifles. 1. M-1 when clean fires perfectly, 8 shots before you have to touch anything but the trigger. 2. Carbine, when clean fires perfect - 15 rounds before you do anything (but pull the trigger). 3. O-3 (The Army's old Springfield or British Enfield - bolt action.) Fires regardless of dirt, grit, etc., as long as it is physically possible to slam the bolt home. 1.1. M-l when dirty has to be worked by hand just like O-3. 2.2. Carbine also must be worked by hand when dirty. Remarks: As long as the M-l and Carbine are clean it is wonderful, but as soon as they get dirty - and not very dirty either, you must work them by hand. The catch is you never know what is liable to happen."

April 18: Dear Mom and Dad,
"We got off a little early today because we pleased the captain. This morning we had identification of aircraft and physical exercise, it wasn't bad. This afternoon we had physical fitness tests. I did 24 push ups, 300 yard run in 47 seconds, 75 yard pig-y-back with a guy my own weight in 25 seconds, and other stuff, all with G. I shoes, etc., plus combat pack. My average was 85%. Then we took a 4 miles march in 48 minutes. We did this so beautifully that the captain let us off at 4 p.m. ..."

April 20: Dear Mom and Dad,

". . . Yesterday we worked out a squad problem. I had 24 rounds of live ammunition because I was a scout, the others had 16 each. We advanced until they pulled targets. Then we maneuvered around and shot at them. They were about 300 yards away. 12 of us managed to hit all the targets and a total of 64 shots in them, a 39% hits average. Fair shooting."

April 24: Dear Mom and Dad,

"Here it is, one year since I went into the Army. Tonight Charley Prentiss and Borkowski and I went to Paris (Texas) to get stuff we needed. For some reason we went to a café and ordered 3 steaks, and then sat down and went over the Army and the War. . . . Then we went over how the War has ruined every man's life in this whole world, only thing is, Americans at least, don't care, and don't even know that there is a war on. . . . I know, and Charley and Borkowski both admitted that they didn't know that there was a War on till they came here. . . . I went alone to Dallas the other day. My buddies both mentioned before were on K.P. . . . I went to the Zion Lutheran Church, Missouri Synod. The whole thing was just like ours. I sure enjoyed every minute of it. The sermon was on Christian education being necessary for everyone right from the beginning."

April 25: Dear Mom and Dad,

". . . German POWs were working on our barracks today putting in new screens. . . . When we came up on one of them he was right in the barracks. Of course he had to be, to get the screens. Well, we practically ran over him. Our rifles were laying all over but they never so much as seemed to look at them. Remember, no-one was guarding any of these guys. . . . A boy named Weinberg asked a German how he was doing, in German. He answered back in German, that he was doing O.K. Then Weinberg asked how he liked it. He said he had been here 6 months and enjoyed it a lot. We aren't suppose to talk to them but they all seem to be nice guys."

April 28: Dear Mom and Dad,

"Lots has happened since Wednesday. Yesterday we went for a full day of demonstrations. First thing was a grenade launcher, then bazooka. We saw it shoot close up. It goes swish and then wham. It makes a hole about the size of a lead pencil in a steel plate. It is supposed to be a secret how it works. . . . We then saw 60 mm and 81 mm mortars work. You can watch the shells fly through the air, they sure look funny. I guess Dad knows how they work. (My Dad had been in World War I.)

*Nazi Village*

Increments, or packages of powder on the fin assembly are for range differences. You have a chart which tells you how many to leave in place so that the shell will go a certain distance (when shot at a certain angle). We saw all the Infantry weapons, including pyrotechnics. They have a pipe like thing that they shot them off with. You hit it on the ground and away they go. Today we attack the Nazi Village. It is the nearest thing to combat anyone can get. We had live ammunition, dynamite charges, machine guns, fire crackers for grenades, pyrotechnics for signaling, walkie-talkies to keep up communications."

April 30: Dear Mom and Dad,
"This morning I went to church again. The sermon was on the 3 questions that Pilate asked Christ. It led to a conclusion that truth was in Christ, and that without truth we could have no real peace, therefore without Christ and without his teachings which are to be followed we will always suffer."

May 7: Dear Mom and Dad,
"Well, just got back from the worst week of Army life. Here is what happened. Monday - rained cats and dogs, got soaking wet, slept off and on. Tuesday - chased wire. . . . Wednesday, started raining again. . . . Thursday, kept on raining, got colder, my shoes never dried out. Went for 4 days, 4 nights with feet wet. . . . Froze to death, almost. Friday, got a ride 19.6 miles to home. The Infantry is hell, and that is putting it mildly. Well, you don't know how wonderful a bed and barracks can look. . .

"Well, here it is, Saturday. We have been getting

acquainted with tanks (M-4 mediums and M-5 lights) all day. We climbed all over them, found out all we could. The M-4 had a 9 cylinder Continental radial engine. They (tankers) all complained that the engine was too weak for a 31 ton tank.... Well, I have answered all those letters now (five of them). Sure haven't had much time lately. How do you like this stationery that is issued by the company?" (See Appendix 2 for an example.)

You might wonder what is meant by "chasing wire." The Signal Corps men put communications wire right on top of the ground. It is used as long as necessary and then picked up and used again. However, in maneuvers, as well as combat, the wire tends to be broken by passing vehicles which don't notice it, or drive over it anyway. In combat it is sometimes broken by shells. So what I meant by "chasing wire" was helping the Signal Corps find and repair breaks in the wire so communications could be re-established.

May 7: Dear Mom and Dad,
"... I didn't tell you before but that storm was the biggest that hit around here in a long time, in fact it flooded everything.... Why I never got a bad cold, or anyone else, I can't understand. Everyone was just tired and very happy to see the good old barracks."

Just when I almost got in big trouble, I don't remember. But I clearly remember the event. We had all "formed up" for a speech by our captain. He told how the Red Cross was a fine organization and that there was a contest to see which outfit would give the most money. He wanted us to win the contest, so he decided that we would each contribute $10 toward this fund. He asked, "Any questions?" I just said something to the effect that I would not be giving as long as I was being told to give, since one of the reasons we were fighting the war was for freedom. I would do what I was told to do as a soldier, but nothing said I had to give for the Red Cross. I can still see what happened. The Captain took on a furious look. Then he turned around for a while. Then he turned back and said, "Men, Mac is right. I have no right to tell you that you have to give. I would appreciate it if you would all give for the Red Cross. Dismissed." From then on I had a higher regard for him than before, and I don't remember that he in any way tried to get even with me for doing as I did.

May 9: Dear Mom and Dad,
**"Nothing much has happened the last two days. Yesterday I was on K.P. Today I didn't do a thing. It seems that because I was on K.P. I didn't get to take a 25 mile hike we had last night. The boys did it from 2200 to 0600 hour this morning, so they got to sleep all day."**

May 11: Dear Mom and Dad,
**"Yesterday we ran a field problem with the tanks from C Company 788th Armored Force, with the 371st Field Artillery, and 394th Anti-tank company. It was very realistic, because only live ammunition was used. In the first phase our mortars shelled the enemy along with our M-l, B.A.R. (Browning Automatic Rifle), and machine gun fire. From there we followed a rolling barrage put down with 105's from the Field Artillery. The shells dig in pretty deep before they go off so I don't see that they are very effective. In the last phase we fired on silhouette tar-**

gets with our weapons. . . . the artillery fired rounds also that burst about 50 yards above the ground. It sprayed the M-4 General Sherman tanks but didn't hurt them, just knocked some periscopes out. . . . It was all pretty realistic and very instructive. Two generals and two Colonels told us later what we did right or wrong."

Major General Walter Lauer, our Commanding General, writes about the training we received at Camp Maxey and in part says, "It was during these months too that all troops experienced their first maneuvers using live mortar and artillery shells in overhead fire. It was a dangerous phase of training but one that was essential. It did not pass without accident, for it was at this time that a short round fell with fatal results among our men advancing in mock attack. The heroic actions of those closely involved, the coolness, speed and precision with which everything humanly possible was promptly accomplished to meet this disaster, further marked the readiness of the command for combat." (p. 100)

May 14: Dear Mom and Dad,
"How was Mother's Day? We are on the alert, so we can't leave camp. . . . Charley Prentiss was transferred to the Antitank company that is across the street. He likes the bigger guns. They use 57 mm pieces. . . . The tanks in the Infantry are driven by tank men. That's all I know. I guess they are attached to the 99th. . . . Prentiss is here with a 45 pistol. He is pretty happy over his new position. The work isn't near as hard as in the regular Infantry."

May 20: Dear Mom and Dad,
"We have been out on the field as enemy since Monday morning at 0700. Here is what we did: Monday - got up at 0400 started out at 0500 got to rear area at 0700 about 6 miles out. We dug in and stayed around until 1500. We then went to the position we were to hold from the 'blues'. All this time, from morning on, P-40's (enemy planes) dove over us. Made it pretty realistic. Reconnaissance planes buzzed around also...."

"Tuesday - We were moved to the reserved line where fox holes had already been dug. It was out on an open field, so we didn't appreciate it much. We had been in the forests before. We didn't do anything else but catch up on lost sleep. Wednesday - We did little or nothing all day.... We went a 1/2 mile in front of our front line to watch for 'enemy.' Nothing happened. Thursday - at about 1600 we saw them coming in large numbers. We phoned back then fired on them (with blanks of course) and retreated to our lines and our old positions. Thursday night Sgt. Dudley took a patrol out. I wasn't on it but here is what is happened. At night it is easy to walk through lines. You sit by the road near the 'enemy' and pretty soon someone will come along. A guard will challenge and you will listen and then learn the pass word. From then on you go forward, knowing the pass word you get through their lines. They found out who was where; etc., and everything else. Coming back to our lines they ran into some fellows that wanted to know who they were. Dudley lied and said Company E of the 393rd (he knew what area he was near.) The guys (enemy of course) said they had been looking all over for that company, so Dudley said follow me and I'll take you to them. Well, he marched them right to our lines, where they soon realized that they were prisoners. It sure made them mad. Friday at 0130 Corporal Boyle and other guys and I went out to find some persons who were behind our lines tapping the wires (connecting to our phone lines). We could not find them. At 0240 we were given prisoners to take to Battalion headquarters. They had been captured almost a mile behind their own lines. They were mad, especially because they had maps that noted all of their defense positions. It showed how well we were doing, and how badly they were.

"As usual everyone came through without getting sick, etc. The attacking force had 6 casualties out of about 4,000 men. One man kicked a dud and we heard it blew him up and killed him, while a Lieutenant's arm was blown off and 6 others were scratched up. One man jumped into a fox hole and a snake bit him. A truck went off a hill and killed another man."

You have read General Lauer's account of our live-ammunition training, and now mine. I wonder which gives the right story. I clearly remember us talking about how dumb it was for a guy to kick what he must have thought was a dud.

May 28: Dear Mom and Dad,
"I went to church this morning. It only lasted 35 minutes. The preacher said (in effect),'be a good little boy.' I don't like that kind of sermon."

May 30: Dear Mom and Dad,
"Yesterday morning we didn't do so terribly much. In the afternoon we had aircraft identification and then a problem with live ammunition. We did not do too well. We have a good squad leader, Sgt. Davies, or we wouldn't have done as well as we did. We have 2 eight-balls that dragged us down. Last night we went on a little problem. Of course it rained and I got my feet soaked. I was a messenger. Had to take messages, oral, between Commanding officers and one of the Lieutenants. It was O.K. It was no use trying to lay down because 3 mosquitoes would come along and hold you down while another one would light on you and bite. These Texas mosquitoes are really powerful creatures. I think they got the plans for the B-24's from them. (Just kidding.)"

June 1: Dear Mom and Dad,
"We came in early today to have a Regimental parade. We are going to have a night problem tonight so we ought to be off tomorrow. So long, Bill"

June 3: Dear Mom and Dad,
"Here it is Saturday again. I was chosen to go to sniper school, so yesterday and today we have been studying different things. We use the Springfield O-3 A3 rifle. A bolt action rifle with a telescope mounted on it. The telescope really brings things up close. The extreme accurate range is 1,000 yards, just twice as far as with the M-1. Our instructor is a Lieutenant Benson. He is one swell guy. I think he is the finest officer I ever have known. He uses his own common sense about everything."

June 4: Dear Mom and Dad,
"Today I have been helping the Supply Sergeant get ready for an ordinance and quartermaster inspection. All equipment has to be displayed. We set out 142 M-1's, 25 carbines, 10 pistols, 3 mortars, 1 50-caliber machine gun, 6 30-caliber machine guns, 13 pairs of binoculars, 3 O-3 rifles, 9 B.A.R's, 6 walkie-talkies, 4 Bazookas, 25 compasses, etc. It took us about 5 hours to place everything out."

June 6: Dear Mom and Dad,
"Well, big things happened today I guess. At about 12 midnight the guys came in from a night problem. They said that they had heard that the invasion had started so the radios went on. Sure enough, they had started." (Reference is to the D-Day landing of our troops on the Normandy beaches.)

June 8: Dear Mom and Dad,
"We fired for record today with the O-3 and the telescopic sight. Maybe Dad can explain why that sight seems to make for inaccuracy. I know I didn't fire well enough to make sniper. I didn't see many guys make it. You have to fire and hit 88 out of 100. Miss one target and you are almost out, 2 and you are. I only missed one completely, but it took a few extra shots to hit some of the rest of the targets. They were at ranges from 200-400 yards. Not bad, but they were the small, not the large targets. . . . After taking everything into consideration I am convinced that the M-1 is the better rifle. The class A rifle will fire with all kinds of dirt in it. The reason I changed was that even the O-3 will get stuck. You will not be able to push the rounds up so when you pull the trigger noth-

ing happens. All I can say is that you will have to be darn careful in combat or something won't go off and it will be T.S. - hum, forgot myself but it does express the situation."

June 14: Dear Mom and Dad,
"I am at the Service Club here at camp. It is a very nice place. I wish that I had come here before. . . . Tell Dad 'Happy Birthday'. I suppose I should send something, but I sure don't know what. If you can get him something, it will be O.K. with me if you take some of that $50.00."

June 18, Dear Mom and Dad,
"We just returned from our attack on permanent field fortifications. I guess we did O.K. They had 30 caliber machine guns, and 61 mm mortars helping us. . . . A guy took a flame thrower and burned out the pill box, then another fellow put explosives inside the box and that did it. All the stuff was real so it made it pretty interesting."

(Comment: As I now think of my parents reading this I cannot help but think that it must have been very upsetting to them. At least it is upsetting to me to realize what they probably thought. I can just see my dad thinking, "That kid of mine doesn't know what he is getting into.") I could continue to quote large portions of letters, but now I will pick up a few highlights, since after June 6, 1944, and the landing in France, our training took on a certain urgency. All the letters began Dear Mom and Dad.

June 23:
**"We have been told to send all our extra stuff home."**

June 27 and we heard about the G-I Bill, so I wrote,
 **"How do you like that bill they passed, $500 for tuition and $50 a month for subsistence? I might go back to school for that."**

A few days after this I was allowed to go home to Pasadena on furlough. After the furlough, Dad and Mom, along with Jean and Jack and me, went to the Pasadena Santa Fe train station so I could go back to duty. We got there, and we really did not know what to say to each other.

At last it came time to go, so I boarded the train and took a seat where I could look out and see the family and wave to them. A soldier was sitting across from me. He said, "Take a good look. It might be the last time you see them." I knew just what he meant. My dad had said they would try to meet us at the train crossing on Allen Ave.
He worked for the post office, knew the train schedule inside and out, and was sure he could make the crossing before the train. Sure enough, they were there as we went by, and so we waved to one another again.

*Me, taken while on vacation*

Realizing now what I had written them, and the war situation, I wonder what they were thinking. Knowing how my mother would speak of me when she would talk to close friends, I can just imagine my Mom thinking, "I wonder if I will ever see my 'little Billy Boy' again."

Getting back to Camp Maxey, Texas, I wrote on July 24: **"I got to camp at 1500 Sunday. . . . I met a Mr. Coiner in Brownswood, Texas. He asked me to stay with him in his Pullman car. He let me have his bunk, so I slept good one night. We talked for quite a while."** July 28: **"We practiced having a parade for General Lauer."** August 3rd I wrote: **"I hope Jean and Jack both had a nice birthday,"** (One has a birthday on August 3rd, the other on the 4th.) August 5th: I tell of having an Infantryman test which included: (1) Medical—emphasis on drinking plenty of water when you have to take a sulfa tablet, (2) Individual protection - about digging a fox hole, etc., (3) Firing weapon, (4) Compass work, (5) Bayonet course, (6) Grenade course, (7) Military courtesy (8) 25-mile hike. I also mention parading for General Lauer. **"He is a rugged looking soldier for a Major General. . . . Quite a few guys passed out in the parade today. The heat was just too much for them. So far I haven't managed to get that bad off."** August 10th: I note that I had glasses to fit in my gas mask. August 14: I had gone to Dallas over the weekend. The stationery is from Hotel Southland. August 16: **"I guess you can see that I cut off the top of the Stationery. They told us to cut off all unit designation. You can see we were about to go overseas."** August 18, I talk about **"a really interesting communications thing. It is just 2 phones connected by a very fine wire. You can hear very well** up to 880 yards, and all you have to do is speak into the phones. It is a pure voice set, (no batteries)." (This would later be the type phone we used on the front lines. It would turn out to be a lifesaver.)

August 23: "Last night I had guard (duty) again for the first time in over a year. . . . They finally got down to putting down who is going to be sniper and who not. Mings and two other fellows are the permanent ones. Two others and I are extras." August 29: "Everything seems to be going O.K., but sort of coming to an end. . . . All patches were removed from clothing. . . . Yes, the war seems to be going pretty good. I just hope they quit darn soon." September 1: I write from Hotel Adolphus and mention that Borkowski and Senft are along since "accidentally we got a 3 day pass." Also, "Our company is now up to full strength." September 5: "Yesterday we all went to a school of scouting and patrolling." September 6: "I'm working in the orderly room today while the regular Mail Orderly Clerk is now away on a three day pass." September 9: "I'm still working in the orderly room. . . . I got a new rifle today. The other one was called unserviceable because it stopped working automatically, and ordnance couldn't change this condition. So last night from 7-12 I cleaned cosmolean off my new rifle. The rifle fired perfectly this morning. It really is a beauty." September 16: "The little lull in writing was caused by a slight change in location to somewhere on the East Coast. . . . That hurricane came along just ahead of us. . . ."

## TRIP TO CAMP MYLES STANDISH, MASSACHUSETTS
## SEPTEMBER 15-17, 1944

## AT CAMP MYLES STANDISH
## SEPTEMBER 18-28, 1944

A letter dated September 18, 1944, is all cut up by a censor. He did leave a diagram in which I had pictured how the bunks we slept in on the train were perpendicular to the direction of travel, and my comment that they were very comfortable.

September 19:
**"I went to the Service Club last night. They have one here that is a regular palace compared to others. The library is as fine as many cities boast. Saw a moving picture of the Tuna fishing off California. It made me wish I was out there with them again.** (A reference to my having in the past gone to Long Beach or Newport Beach to go deep sea fishing with friends.) **It was always great fun. . . . Did you read General Marshall's speech? He said that 8 more Divisions were going to be sent overseas this month. I just wonder who they could be. . . ."**

What had happened, that I could not mention before, was this. We had gotten aboard trains at Camp Maxey, Texas, and traveled across the top parts of the states of Louisiana, Alabama, and Georgia and then gone up the east coast to Camp Myles Standish, just outside Boston. In 1945, I wrote: **"The trip up to Camp Miles Standish was okay and spent mostly in looking at the** scenery of the South and East as we passed through. Washington, D.C. and New York City looked big and wonderful. The guys were still saying that we aren't going over seas. If we do, we will just go to occupy some place. It is always easier to say no to something than to face the facts. That is the way with something you don't want to believe." At Miles Standish we were given lectures on what we were going to do, censorship, travel on a boat, and how to get off a boat if it was hit. They kept us in shape with drill and lots of walks and calisthenics.

One thing I still remember about our trip to Miles Standish is the train stop in Roanoke, Virginia. We all got off the train and went through about a half-hour of calisthenics. I suppose I remember it because we attracted a big crowd of people who then applauded us when we got back on the train.

## TRIP TO ENGLAND
## SEPTEMBER 29-0CTOBER 11, 1944

September 29: Dear Mom and Dad,
"We put all that equipment plus some Gas Clothing in our packs and bags and took a trip to Boston harbor. Here the Red Cross gave us coffee and donuts and let us go aboard the ship. The girls got a lot of last minute kidding and joking that the fellows had stored up. There was lots of laughing and hollering because I guess no-one wanted to face the fact that when you got aboard a ship it wasn't just for a pleasure cruise. The ship was the U.S.S. Excelsior, a class 3 cargo ship. It could make about 22 knots and carry 2,200 men and crew. It had 4 or 5 holds. The bunks

**were 6 or 8 high and the aisles between bunks so close that your shoulders scraped bunks each side of you. That sure was packing us in."**

Company A was put on MP (Military Police) duty for the trip over. We saw to it that no one went where they weren't supposed to. The ship got under way on the night of September 29 with the 394th aboard with some attached units. We watched the lights of Boston disappear into the night. I wondered if I would ever see them again. Ison was on watch with me. He said, "Better take a good look. It might be a long time before we see it again, if ever." I can remember wondering more and more as to why this war had come about and so disrupted all our lives.

**"The next day we found ourselves in the midst of a big convoy of 13 ships carrying troops, and 47 carrying cargo. We noticed some tankers with airplanes on their decks, and they and us being in the center of the convoy. The regular cargo ships were around us. Near evening we noticed that we were constantly changing positions (zigzagging) and that there were 10 distinct columns of ships with a destroyer escort at the head of each. Other escorts were at our sides and one to the rear."** The next day we realized we must have joined many ships at night, for we found ourselves in the midst of a convoy of hundreds of ships. There were ships as far as the eye could see in every direction. I have two letters written at sea. One has stamped on it, "Passed by U.S. Army Examiner 44132." Then it is signed in beautiful handwriting, Martin L. Hay, 2nd Lt.

In this letter I write:
"You should have seen some of these sea sick cases we had. I always thought that Jack got pretty sick but some of the fellows here really have him beat. One Lieutenant was the worst I think that I saw. He got so white that it looked like he was surely going to die. The bad part of it was that he stayed that way for about four days. I saw him today and he seems O.K. I guess you remember me mention Mings. He has been sick just about all the way. The only thing is that he doesn't look bad at all. The way I found out was when he asked me if there were any way back by land. When I said "no," he glumly told me that after the war he was going to settle down in Europe. Food aboard this ship is pretty good. The only thing is that we only get two meals a day. At those two meals they give you enough food to last you two days. No one was ever that hungry so an awful lot of food was thrown away. This Army sure does act in a mysterious way at times. . . . Well, I'm convinced of one thing right now, it is darn hard to write a letter when everything that is really interesting is on the taboo list. Now that I look at this letter and see how much I've gotten on it, I'm wondering if you can even read it. Guess I had better quit. So long, Bill"

I found one V-Mail letter from our time on board the ship, but undated, which says:

Dear Mom and Dad,
"I suppose you have been wondering why I haven't written you in so long. Well, it seems that they don't have a way of picking mail up at sea. So far I haven't gotten sea sick. We went through a little rough weather, but now it is nice and calm. I think that

**some of those fishing trips Art and I went on were lots worse than we have hit so far, though it sure was bad enough.** (Art Ude, my best friend in Pasadena, CA.) **You could always manage the decks and walk them so I figure that isn't too bad. - Our platoon has guard aboard ship from 8-12 day and 8-12 at night. It gives us plenty of time on deck. It really is more of a pleasure than a job because we get to see more and also be on deck long. I think fresh air has a lot to do with keeping sea-sickness away. So long, Bill"**

The trip across was fairly uneventful, except for three things: (1) The day before we saw land, air planes began flying over us. (2) We were told that the escort ships had picked up indications of a submarine. We heard explosions and then the clang of the pressure waves as they hit the ship. They had depth charged a submarine, but if there really was one, it got away. (3) Just short of land our ship dropped out of the convoy and the crew of the 5-inch gun mounted on the rear of the ship got a little practice shooting.

## BRIDGEPORT, ENGLAND
## OCTOBER 11-NOVEMBER 2, 1944

We were in England for several weeks. The Story of the 394th Infantry, prepared by 394th Infantry Special Services, 1st Lt. Walton T. Farrar, Special Service Office, and Pfc. James L. Haseltine, Editor, says that we arrived in Liverpool, England, on October 11, 1944. My distinct memory of that event is of walking on deck and finding we were in a dense fog. As it lifted we looked around to see only the masts and superstructures of many sunken ships in the harbor. For some reason we were not immediately taken off the ship, but on October 13 we did go off and were put aboard English-type trains that appeared like toys to us, since they were so much smaller than the trains we were used to in the U.S. But these "toy trains" went through England at a rapid rate. When we arrived at Dorsetshire, southern England, our company was trucked to Bridgeport, England, a town nearby. We remained there until November 2, and then in stages moved from there to Southampton, to arrive in LeHavre, France, on November 6, 1944. I wrote several letters home during this time, and since they give a good picture of what we did while in England, I will quote from a few of them.

October 14: Dear Mom and Dad.,
**"We are at the present time somewhere in England. The trip across wasn't enjoyed by some, but personally I enjoyed it very much. We have been told not to say where we started from, where we landed, etc. ... We went through several towns that showed signs of being bombed. The English had all the rubble cleaned away though. . . . The food has been O.K. so far. We ate K rations the other day, C for another, and now it is back to plain ordinary food."**

October 15: Dear Mom and Dad,
**"I received your letter dated the 26th today, and was glad to hear from you. . . . The first day here the English children asked and received from us gum, candy, oranges, and some sugar that we had. It seemed O.K. at the time, but now every time we walk down the street they beg for things as if they were starving. They aren't anywhere near starving around here. . . . Everyone rides bikes here. Old, middle aged and young. Horses and carts are far from rare, and automobiles are used, but mostly by businesses**

that demand them. We are having a little trouble with the left side of the road travelling, but not too much. So long, Bill"

October 18: Dear Mom and Dad,
"Everything is going O.K. with me here in England. I sort of miss having the Ice Cream and other foods we have for sale at our P.X.'s back home. About the only thing we can buy is Fish and Chips (Fish and French fries - English style.) That's O.K. but I still like ice cream. To keep us out of mischief they are taking us on hikes. The hikes aren't so terribly long, but they go up and down hills which makes it terribly hard compared to walking on the level."

October 20: Dear Mom and Dad,
"Things are still status quo. They had us sew our division patches back on. I guess so everyone would know who we were. We went to an awful lot of trouble to keep anyone from finding out who we were, and now they put our insignia back on. It beats me. . . . Yesterday I was on guard duty and had quite a few things of interest come up. First was that everyone that came past the gate said 'good-morning', not just a few people but everyone that came past. Of course I said 'good-morning' in return to keep up our international relations. (While in Bridgeport we were housed in homes right in town in the midst of homes occupied by civilians)."

General Lauer writes about our stay in Bridgeport:

"The thoughtful courtesy of the English country folk, their fatalistic attitude toward life, their set customs and peculiar class distinctions, and their entire mode of life with few modern conveniences were a revelation to these American lads. Visits with courtesy food packages when invited to share a meal at home with these stalwart and staunch folk who were being strictly rationed and yet wished to share their limited food with their visitors to show their appreciation of the great task these newcomers were taking over, quickly established a mutual bond of friendship and understanding." *(p.105)*

October 22: Dear Mom and Dad,
**"Tomorrow some of us are supposed to get 48 hour passes to London, so I might have something to tell you, that is; if a buzz bomb doesn't get us. The little I saw of Bristol I got the impression that quite a few bombs had landed there. One block was a neat row of foundations."**

October 26: Dear Mom and Dad,
**"Everything still goes O.K. Monday and Tuesday I was in London spending a 48 hour pass which I came back late on. We got back about 8 hours late so we have been restricted to the barracks for 5 days. It was our fault so I can't make up much of an excuse except to say that next time I'll find out when the train comes back and not take someone else's word for it. Here is what happened in London. We arrived at Paddington station about 2 p.m. Monday afternoon. We took the Underground (Subway) to Piccadilly Circus, just where a lot of streets come together, no circus, and went to the Red Cross Rainbow corner. Here they sent us to the Washington Club for rooms. They sent us to 22 Audley St. for a room. The room was nice, in fact wonderful considering it only cost 2 shillings for overnight. We then**

went and had supper at a place. We had a pretty good meal, but not anything like the states. They serve a lot of starchy food for lack of fresh foods and meat. We then went to a Newsreel theater, then back to the hotel. We talked with an English boy that was just about to be drafted into the British army. We explained to him our money system, and told him that gangsters didn't run around and shoot up everything and lot of other stuff. It sure is funny the way the Englishmen think about us, and as far as that goes, we about them. . . . Trafalgar Square is where the statue of Lord Nelson stands. Saw it several times. It is on the way to Parliament, Downing Street, Big Ben, etc. Along the side of the House of Lords stands a statue of Richard the Lion Hearted. He must have had a close call with a bomb, because he is badly chipped up, and so is his horse."

October 28: Dear Mom and Dad,
"For the last week we haven't done too much of interest. We live in an English home. There are 2-12 in a room depending on room size. Ours has 5. We have a little heater and other comforts that make it O.K. Being in town we are all making quite a few friends. When on guard the children come and talk to us. . . . A lady across the street insists on giving us tea about 10:30 every day. We always accept to keep up international relations. She thinks an awful lot of the Americans, and we don't want to discourage her. . . . So long, Bill"

October 30: Dear Mom and Dad,
"I went to town tonight and saw the movie

Rembrandt, with Charles Laughton. I thought that it was a pretty good show.... I'm sending this money order for Christmas. Buy whatever you think is best with it for 'you all' for Christmas... Several days ago a Red Cross mobile unit hit town, so we decided that we were in for some good American Coffee and donuts. Well, right after chow the other day we fell out in formation and marched up and received our donuts.... The officers were around telling you what to do and making remarks of different sorts, and in all disgusting everyone. I guess the Army never will realize that you like to get away from the Army idea when you are doing such things."

## INTO BATTLE
## NOVEMBER 3 - DECEMBER 15, 1944

November 10: Dear Mom and Dad, "We are now somewhere in Belgium. We got a nice little ride across France and into a Belgium farmyard. The first night we slept on the ground. It started to snow etc., so we have moved into a hay loft. I slept better last night than I have since I've been in the E. T. O. (European Theater of Operations.) The hay is really nice and soft and warm.... During pretty good weather we see or hear buzz bombs going over. If they go right overhead it

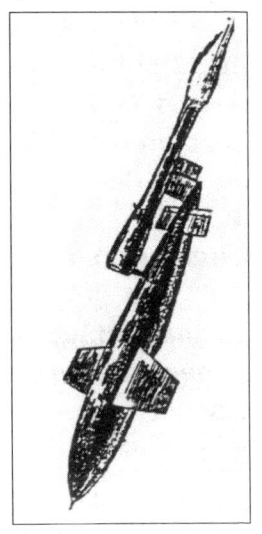

*Buzz Bomb—A German V-I unmanned flying bomb*

**sounds like 10 bombers going over low. These buzz bombs are really noisy. . . . Well, I can write again. Today is the 13th, and the snow is about a foot deep. Personally I haven't suffered too much. . . . We have rabbits, chickens, cows, pigs and other animals running around the place we are staying. We are still somewhere in Belgium, and still the buzz bombs come over. . . . Don't be expecting me home too soon. I sure would come home in a hurry if I could, but the war isn't over yet."**

The official history of the 394th Infantry Regiment of the 99th Infantry Division records that we boarded ships around November 4, crossed the English channel and arrived in Le Havre, France, which is at the mouth of the Seine River, on November 6, 1944.

I recorded many of my war experiences after the war, while in Furth, Germany, with the occupation troops. The following is largely taken from this account and begins at the time we prepared to cross the channel into France.

On November 3, 1944, came the order to put on long johns, OD's (olive drab wool clothing), and pack the other stuff up. We then walked about 2 miles to the railroad station and got aboard trains. The walk just about killed us; not quite though. We got to Southampton in a short time and then walked a long way to an English ship, which we boarded. It looked like any other freighter but reeked with the smell of sheep. We got aboard nevertheless. Our quarters were a dining hall—where we slept, ate, and existed. It was so crowded that it was almost impossible for everyone to lie down to sleep. No cots were provided. We began to wonder if we were the forgotten troops. Arriving in Le Havre we found that the entire waterfront was level with the ground for a half mile inland, and all the pieces of land that jutted out to form inlets were level too. Just a bunch of cement blocks and a few twisted girders were all that we could see. We went over the side of the ship by means of a steel ladder into amphibious ducks. These were large, open, 4-wheeled vehicles with a propeller that pushed them through the water. They were so low in the water that I was sure the water would come over the edges, but little did. They ran up on the shore and we disembarked with all our equipment.

After a half-mile walk we got on trucks which took us to a place about five miles east of nearby Forges, France. There we disembarked from the trucks and pitched our two-man shelter half-tents and stayed overnight. During the night a snowy rain fell, which made us absolutely miserable, and turned everything into a gooey mess. In the morning we left our tents for breakfast. Coming back, we soon noticed that we were missing things. We had seen some French kids walking around but had thought little of it. Now we realized they had helped themselves to what they wanted. The fact that these kids would steal from us did not set well. If they really were so much in need, why not ask? But, to steal from us after what our armed forces had done in freeing them from the Nazis seemed a very thankless, low down, deed.

Then it started raining. The whole area soon went from bad to worse. All this time we were without any proper protection against water getting into our boots. Until now we had not been issued overshoes, so our feet got wet, and many complained about how miserable they were. We had rubbed grease into the leather of the boots, but this did not keep the water out. We were a bunch of woebegone GI's, especially as it now began to snow.

In spite of the situation, we were told to take down our shelter half-tents and prepare to leave. We got aboard trucks and then traveled 285 miles along the top of France and finally to Aubel, Belgium. (Aubel is a small farming town north of Verviers, in the eastern-most portion of Belgium near the Liege-Aachen Highway.) There we pitched our shelter half-tents in a beautiful snow-covered pear orchard. The pear trees, without any leaves, standing all in neat rows, made an enchanting picture. I am sure we would have all enjoyed the situation if only we had had a nice home in which to stay, our feet had been dry, and we were not at war.

It rained and snowed until finally we were all pretty wet. As it would soon be dark, they decided something had to be done. The Belgian farmer allowed us to sleep in his hay barn. We got all our equipment together and moved in. The whole platoon got into one barn. It was plenty crowded but it was better than being outside. Of course the hay slowly begin to absorb equipment. One of the fellows lost a part of his rifle he was cleaning. They issued us each a dry blanket for the night. With that and a sleeping bag we got our first good night's sleep in a long while. We all slept with our clothes on for two reasons: (1) It dried our clothes out, and (2) it was a lot warmer that way.

I'll never forget eating breakfast the next morning. In the Army during war time you always must carry your rife and wear your web belt (with bayonet, canteen, first aid kit, and entrenching tool attached), and that means at chow time too.  So we went out to chow with our rifles (barrel down) over our right shoulder, our web belt and attached equipment in place, our raincoats on, and mess gear in hand.  It was raining, and it was still dark.  We stood in line, slowly went forward, and finally got our chow, plus rain water added to same.  Then it slowly got light enough to see some distance, and we all got a laugh.  We were all standing around eating, not being able to find a dry spot to sit, and standing around something we suddenly realized was a great big pile of manure.

On November 14, our 394th Infantry Regiment finally went on line in the Weisserstein-Losheimergrabben sector, relieving the 60th Infantry Regiment of the 9th Infantry Division which had landed on D-Day.  So the official regimental history says, "In the records, the combat history of the 394th began on Nov. 14, 1944, when the regiment went on line in the Ardennes."  As we neared the front, Captain Blatch told everyone to be quiet; he didn't want the enemy to hear us.  Haefner had a cold and kept coughing, so the Captain kept saying, "Stop that noise."  Well, of course it was impossible for Al (Haefner's first name was Alfred) to keep from coughing.  Then suddenly the Captain slipped and fell.  In the darkness no one noticed it until a couple more had fallen over him.  Then there really was noise. The column stopped so we took a break.  We moved on and turned a corner to hear a cheerful, "Hi Joe," which was our Captain's first name.  We then noticed that big fires were burning, with men standing around them.  It was obvious that the Germans weren't very close.  All the Captain's worries were for nothing.  But we realized he meant well and was as nervous as we were about what lay ahead.

Sgt. Gribes, our platoon sergeant led us to our area. Our platoon leader, Lt. Thompson, gave us the big picture. It seemed we were to be in reserve. The front line was 300 or 400 yards ahead through the forest, with the Germans perhaps a mile in front of that. Being in reserve we would have to furnish men for patrols, front and rear. REAR? Yes, the rear area was to be patrolled to see if the Jerries (German soldiers) were getting back of the front line.

The 9th Division boys had dug holes about 3 or 4 feet into the ground, bedded the bottom with pine boughs and hay, put logs over the top, and a shelter half over that. Our home, Senft's and mine, was a pretty good one, at least dry. The outside ground was wet and soggy with snow but we were okay in our hole. We put our equipment on the log roof under our shelter halfs. Our days became pretty much the same. In the morning chow was brought to us from Wirtzfeld. We spent our time chopping wood for the fire and trying to keep dry. It either was snowing or raining all the time. We found that we were in a buzz bomb alley. Ten or twelve over every night, shaking the ground and making a great noise. A few lit near us, and the artillery boys shot down a few, but the majority went on to their targets. Our regimental history says, *"Buzz Bomb Alley* **was the title soon bestowed on the 394th's sector, as the robombs began to sputter over the treetops in an almost endless stream, spitting their orange flame. Ack-Ack crews accounted for some of the bomb-on-wings. Others crashed into the regimental area or sped on to blast Eupen, Liege, Malmedy, Verviers, Antwerp, and other rear-area cities."**

I am amazed at what I wrote home at the time. Now, fifty-plus years later I have no recollection at all of writing some of what I wrote. Some examples:

November 15, Dear Mom and Dad,
"We are still in Belgium, but in a different spot. We are about as close to the Germans as we can get without them being able to shoot us with a rifle. The buzz bombs still go over, thank goodness, though one did land pretty close. . . . When Ison and I were looking for fire wood we came on a cleared field and a big forest across the way. It looked just like some of these Christmas cards. Fir trees covered with snow from top to bottom and just standing there as if they were posing for a picture. We kept still and it all seemed to be in a dream world. Really nice, and it made the war sort of out of place. I'm writing this letter in front of a wood fire and listening to the guys chew the rag. A minute ago they tried to take one of the best guys in our squad out and put him into another company. He isn't so much a soldier, but you can bet your life that as long as he is around everyone will be in good spirits and humor and that counts a lot whether some people think so or not. . . . So long, Bill"

November 18: Dear Mom and Dad,
"Here I am, lying on my belly in a dugout, with a fir log 2 inches over my head, a candle for light, and a guy named Senft beside me doing the same thing. In this position I have read your letters of the 1st, 2nd, and 3rd. I would write during daylight but there just doesn't ever seem to be enough time. If you want to know what we are part of, I think it is the 1st Army.

**It cleared up today and the snow melted from the tree tops. It got lots of my stuff wet. . . . Here is a little slip of paper I found in a wood shed where I slept one night. I don't know what it says. It seems to be dated 1931."**

(Not until I was in Tacoma, Washington, in 1999 for the high school graduation of our granddaughter Kami Brown did I have the note translated. I was introduced to Mrs. Adelheid Waller, who had been brought up in Germany in the 30s and gone through the war there. She translated the slip, and it turns out that it was a little notice from a newspaper publisher saying that they could not be expected to return the subscription price of the paper if there were a strike, lockout, etc. Mrs. Waller then volunteered the information that many people over the years had asked her how the Germans had fallen for Hitler. She pointed out that Hitler brought stability and prosperity to Germany. Naturally they thought he was a great leader, since the Germans had suffered from 1918 till 1931 through all kinds of troubles. It was not till later that they realized that he was a bad man. But by then he had control of the government. So what could they do?)

November 24: Dear Mom and Dad,
**"I'll have to tell you first about our Thanksgiving dinner. They really outdid themselves to get us turkey, sweet potatoes, gravy, peas, cauliflower, cabbage, cake, and peaches. Lots of it too. We ate it in a drizzling rain, but if you thought of home it was O.K . . . ."**

What I did not write home was that about this time all of us got deathly sick. We were so violently ill that when we were not throwing up the food we had eaten, we were running to the slit trenches and relieving ourselves as if our guts were going to come out. If the Germans had attacked at this time, we would have been absolutely helpless. Of course, the big shots were very upset, wondering what had happened. They checked and found that the water we were using to sanitize our mess gear was not hot enough. So, we had contaminated food in our mess gear, and eating that, we all had gotten food poisoning. Picture the situation, and you can see the problem. At that time we were eating regular food, prepared by our cooks. They would come out and we would walk by, and they would put the meat, potatoes, peas and carrots, etc., in our mess gear. We would eat. Then we would clean our gear by scraping off any excess food and then going by a regular metal garbage can that was filled with water, supposedly to be boiling hot. But the weather was very cold, sometimes below freezing. As we each put our now-cold aluminum mess gear into the water, it had a cooling effect. The result was that the water did not stay hot enough to sanitize our mess gear, and so what happened was that we were actually poisoning ourselves. (A gasoline-fired water heater heated the water, but it could not do the job.)

Our first patrol was on November 25, an ambush patrol. We slipped into position at dusk along a trail and got into position. It was 1800. All night we stood or sat in the rain waiting for the Jerries, but none came. It seemed like years before Sgt. Davies and Ison came to see how I was doing. I told them I was freezing and asked what time it was. Only 0300. "I'll die before 0800," I told Sgt. Davies. He showed me how to sit on my helmet, put my raincoat over my head with just my eyes looking out, and told me I would soon be warm. He was right. It was a wonder the way it worked. I was all warm except for my feet in no time. My feet were freezing and I dared not make noise stamping them. Our route back took us along a forest which fronted a wide beautiful valley stretching out to the Germans. Germany really is a beautiful country. One thinks of the words of one hymn verse, "Where every prospect pleases, and only man is vile."

November 26: Dear Mom and Dad,
**"I sent my watch home today. I bounced it off the deck of the ship on the way over here, and it hasn't worked since. There are no repairs up here near the front. So far I've been up to the front lines once. The Siegfried line is in front of us. I guess the whole of the 1st Army faces the line. Those pill boxes look pretty tough. There goes that ack-ack, again. They are shooting at a buzz bomb. The tracers and flack really are beautiful at night. Between the anti-aircraft guns and the artillery, we have quite a serenade. I don't think they mind us saying that we are in back of the front lines. I'm not sure exactly how far but it is quite a walk, an hour at least. The times I went up there were for patrols of different nature. No Germans were sighted... Oh, I'm feeling as good if not better than I ever did before. For some reason you don't seem to catch cold out in this open air. Well, I guess that will be all for now. We are building a log cabin to live in over the winter."**

The idea of a cabin came about this way. We got so tired of being cold and wet that we asked permission to build a cabin to live in. Permission was given. After 2 days work, an order came down for all companies to build a hut for each squad (12 men). Well, we just had a head start. We finished in seven days. A jeep brought in roofing material and stoves. Our official history says, "But Germans weren't the only enemies the GI's had to fight. There was the icy cold of a winter that had to be spent in foxholes, and the ugly crippler, 'trenchfoot.' These were combated by building squad shelter huts, by massaging feet, and by fashioning makeshift stoves."

November 30: Dear Mom and Dad,
**"We held a little celebration today when two of the fellows got packages. We had a feast of candy and cookies. I'm just waiting for those packages you sent. I wish that they would hurry up and get here. . . . By the way, I got a shower and a change of clothes the other day. First time in 3 weeks."**

December 1: "Dear Jean and Jack *(my sister and brother, 17 and 15 at the time),*
**"I thought that I might as well write you two a note. How is school going? I wish you could come over here with me and see what I have seen. It would be a good year's school in a few weeks. The ocean trip was O.K. . . . England, France, and Belgium are all very beautiful countries. The farmers of all three countries seem to be living well. The majority of them have homes the size of mansions, two stories with barns right near or as part of the house. They all seemed to have 12 or so cows and plenty of hay, bikes, toys, lot of clothing and linen. So long, Bill"**

About December 2 or so, Sgt. Davies announced that we were to go on a reconnaissance patrol in order to get information about a German town in front of us named

Losheim. (See Map 1). We were to see if any German soldiers were there, and if present, how many.

We moved out the next morning, after watching the Lieutenant spread a map out in front of Sgt. Davies to show him where we were to go and how to get there. We were not to go directly but in a roundabout way, so if any Germans saw us, they would not guess where we were going. I was first scout, Mings second scout, Sgt. Davies patrol leader, Ison assistant patrol leader, Ketron BAR man, Senft ammunition carrier for the BAR, Seagraves assistant BAR man, and Haefner and the other fellows, riflemen. As scout, I had to go first and wherever Sgt. Davies said. We went this way and that. Time began to go by, and we did not come to the town. We had gone through woods, across fields, and up and down hills. All the time we were very nervous expecting any minute to be spotted and shot at. After all, we were in no man's land, between the two armies. I got more and more nervous because it seemed to me that we were lost. It should not have taken this long to get to the city of Losheim. We only had so much time to make our patrol. We were expected back before dark. The password changed at dark. If we did not get back by then, we would be in big trouble.

At about this time we were walking across a farmer's field. All of a sudden Sgt. Davies called a halt and proceeded to walk out in front of everyone. I couldn't believe what he was doing! We were right out in the open. If anyone saw us we were in the worst possible position. He put the map on the ground. He was about 25 feet in front of me at the time. He got the map in position and looked at it. He looked this way and that. Then he turned to me and motioned for me to come up to where he was. (Remember—when on patrol the men keep spread out, the idea being it will be harder for someone to wipe you out.) I got up to where Sgt. Davies was, and he asked, "Where do you think we are?" He then pointed to a place on that map and said, "I think we are here, and the town should be right over there, but it isn't." I looked at the map. And remember, this is a map which is actually a picture of the land taken from an airplane. I checked first to make sure that the north on the compass and the north on the map were the same. They were. Then I looked around and soon realized where we were. But it was not where he had pointed. I told him, "I believe we are here." He wanted to know how I figured. I then pointed to our left and showed him it was wooded, as was the area to the left of the spot I was pointing at on the map. To our right the ground sloped slowly down to a low area. Beyond and over higher ground was Losheim. Behind us was the forested area we had just come from. He said, "I think you are right. Can you guide us to the town?" I said, "Yes," so off we went.

We went across and down the field to our right, a very slow descent. Getting there who should we see but a dead German soldier. He was the first dead person I had ever seen. He looked so small and insignificant, even though his body was bloated from lying there for some days. I could not help but ask myself if each one of us was so small and so insignificant as this? It was a very sobering moment. "Let's go," said Sgt. Davies, so we went on toward the town. As we came near the top of the rise we noticed something—a barbed wire fence, strung tight. It went to our right and left as far as we could see. We had no wire cutters and were afraid of going over the fence, knowing if we had to make a run for it we would be a very easy target, especially when trying to get over the fence.

"Go to the left along the wire," said Davies. "We'll go around it." We went to the left, and found ourselves going farther and farther. We hit high ground, and looking to our right could now see the town a mile or so away. We could barely see the buildings, really only seeing a church steeple clearly. We looked at the map and saw that a road was just over the top of the slight rise to our left front. Sgt. Davies said to go that way. Personally, I didn't like it. It looked to me as if the wire had been put where it was just to get us to go to that road, thinking it would be the best way. But I went ahead. About half way across, and going a little fast, since high ground is always a dangerous place to be on, I looked back. I immediately put up my hand and yelled, "STOP!" I was in the middle of a mine field that the fellows were just entering. Why I had not stepped on one I will never know, other than to say the Lord was being very good to me. I told Sgt. Davies the situation. He wanted to go on through. I said I believed we could make it if we carefully stretched our heads forward and looked back and made sure of where the mines were and then took a step. It looked as if the shoe mines had been put in this way: a soldier had put a spade into the soil, tilted up the soil, took a little dirt out, throwing it to one side, and then slipped the mine into the space. The result was that you could easily see where the mines were from the German side, since you looked back at the tipped up area. But not from the other side. It looked like a plain grassy area. We all went safely through the mine field and found ourselves on the road leading into the town.

We then went down the road toward the town. A person naturally feels that there is strength in being close to others. So we began to bunch up. Sgt. Davies saw what was happening and yelled at us to maintain separation. He was absolutely right. In combat it is best to maintain good separation. It makes it much harder for someone to shoot down a lot of men if they are spread out. So we spread out and went on toward the town. As we got closer, we realized that we could not see one person, one vehicle, one animal—nothing except finally one chicken. This was mighty strange. We felt like we were under constant observation, and we suspected someone was in the church tower keeping tabs on us. I finally told Sgt. Davies that I did not like the looks of things. I thought we should get out while the getting was good. He said, "I agree. Make a run for it just through the mine field. Then regroup. They cannot see the mine field and will probably not think we will go that way." We all turned and ran. Not too smart really. We got through the mine field, picking up one for a sample to show the officers, when all hell broke lose. Just one artillery shell after another. Just as we thought. We had been under observation. But they were shooting toward the wrong place.

Sgt. Davies came up to me and handed me the map. "Do you think you can get us back?" I looked at the map. We were actually less than a thousand yards away from where we had left. I told him this and he said, "That I don't believe. But lead us in anyway." So we took off, running through the woods toward our front lines. We ran at an angle that I figured would lead us to where we wanted to be. We had not gone far when I stopped, and the fellows wanted to know why I had stopped. I told them, "Because we are only about 150 feet from where we left, and if we run out of these woods the guys will shoot first and asked questions later. We need to shout out the password and carefully work our way in." They did not believe we were that close to our lines. But we went carefully forward and yelled to get someone's attention. When asked, we gave the password. We were then told to come on into the lines. Our officer came forward and asked Sgt. Davies to give him a report. I handed the shoe mine to Sgt. Davies and we went back to our log home. We were mighty thankful to be back.

December 5: Dear Mom and Dad,
"... I got 4 letters today, Nov. 16-20th. All Air Mail, so they made about as good time as the V-Mail's do. Thanks for the clippings, etc. I read very word of them. I'm saving that one about trusting in the Lord and not worrying about things you can't do anything about, etc. That has always sort of been my motto. . . . 'Der Fuerher' seems to have run short of buzz bombs. Very few have come over lately. The A-A boys shot one down the other day, and it landed right on one of our positions. Now they only shoot when the buzz bomb is in a very narrow lane of travel. - If you want to see something beautiful, you ought to see the planes fly over for a raid on Germany. They fly over for hours, high up, with their silver bellies glittering in the sun light. Every clear day we see them, and they really look nice."

December 6: Dear Mom and Dad,
"I sure hope you all have a swell Christmas like we always used to have. We moved into our cabin to-

day, Dec. 6, '44. We have a coal stove that really gives off heat. We don't have a lot of room but it sure is enough to make it O.K. The P.X. store came up today. We got Hershey bars, cookies, and other things. It is nice to get stuff like that every now and then. Everything seems to be going O.K. around here and as always they keep us busy. I wonder what they'll have us do now that our cabins are done. Merry Christmas again, Bill"

December 8: Dear Mom and Dad,
"Not too much has been happening lately. A couple of weeks ago we were on an ambush patrol somewhere out in no man's land. The patrol made us eligible for the Combat Infantry Badge which we were given. That makes $5.00 more per month."

December 9: Dear Mom,
"... Old Hitler must have found a bomb in the cellar, because it is the first buzz bomb that we have heard in about 3 days. - Right now I'm sitting in our log hut, writing while one of the boys is taking a bath in his steel helmet, Sgt. Davies, our squad leader is making coffee before he goes on guard, the rest of the boys are reading, writing, or getting ready to hit the hay. It is all a very happy household in about 10x16 feet. . . . To answer your question. In Bridgeport, England, we stayed in a large private home. We marched to chow which was about 1/4 mile away. . . . The Sibleys sure seem to be doing okay. . . So long, Bill"

December 10, Dear Mom and Dad,
"I thought I'd send the 'Stars and Stripes', our daily newspaper if they can get it to us. We all think it is a

pretty good sheet. - I thought I'd tell you about my first patrol. It seems to be O.K. to tell about it.... (I then relate what you have read above, but in far fewer words.) **I was talking to a jeep driver the other day. He was telling me all about our little patrol. It seems we were pinned down by extensive fire, and had an awful time getting the mine. His captain had the mine he said. Boy, how a story gets blown up.... We told the driver that we were on the patrol and walked away. We didn't want to spoil his story by telling him the real story."**

## BATTLE OF THE BULGE
## DECEMBER 16, 1944 - JANUARY 31, 1945

December 28: Dear Mom and Dad,
**"I'm sorry that I haven't been able to write until now, but all I can say is that I'm awfully thankful that I can write home at all. We had a little battle that I suppose I'll be able to tell you about one of these days. I'm only sorry that we had to go the wrong way. The German's got everything I possessed, G. I. or otherwise, except what I was wearing. They now have your picture and everything else except my wallet, money, and clothes including my overcoat which I was glad to have later. The enclosed German money is off a fellow Mings shot. The German was trying to shoot at me, but Mings saved the day."**

Our "little battle" was the Battle of the Bulge. What I now write about is taken largely from my record of events that I made shortly after the war while in Furth, Germany, but also from an account that I also made in answer to my sister's request for information about my war experiences. I begin this account of the battle by recording events shortly before December 16, the day the battle began.

Between about December 12 and 16, we were given the task of digging better positions for our outpost. An outpost is a dug-in position in front of your main line of defense. (See Map 1) It is maintained day and night with men carefully looking toward the enemy, trying to see what they are doing, and especially if they are about to attack. And since you are anywhere from 50 to 100 yards in front of the main line, you tend to be very alert, knowing if you are not you might end up a prisoner of war, or dead. I record:

*PFC Arthur Mings,*
*By permission:*
*CHECKERBOARD*

"On the 14th we all went up. Mings and I helped on one hole while Ison and Al were on another. Paris, our Platoon runner was out helping Lt. Thompson shoot a deer. Sgt. Jones' platoon was manning the outpost. Gabriel, an old ASTP acquaintance, McNulty and a few others were out on the post when we left at dusk. The Lt. had shot a deer, and he was very happy about it. Ison skinned it for him. It seemed like Ison could do anything. He was around 30, well built, had a wife and four children, and was well liked by everyone."

I asked Ison one day how come he was in our outfit, since married men with four children did not have to be in the infantry. He said he was a coal miner from West Virginia, and where he came from, freedom and the United States of America were very important. He was willing to die for his country so that his children could live in freedom rather than be ruled over by some dictator like Hitler. To this day I can still see him saying this to me as we sat outside my hole there in the forest shortly before the Battle of the Bulge. No one else had ever said anything like that to me. And it was obvious that what he said, he said from the heart.

Ison's "buddy" was usually Scartz, an Italian. He was back at a rest camp at Bullingen getting a shower. I mention this since Ison and Scartz were so unlikely a pair—Scartz so talkative and outgoing, while Ison was such a very sober and reserved person.

Well, we all were dog-tired from digging and then logging in the holes. We used logs to line the edges of these rather large, rectangular shaped holes for added protection. Little Mings—hardly over five feet tall, and who was from Kentucky and constantly chewing tobacco—even said he had done a hard day's work.

We had a great bunch of fellows in that company, and especially our platoon: Meehan and his true loves that he was always telling us about; Long and his Browning Automatic Rifle that he kept so clean; little R. A. Wilson whom we called Monk because of the way he looked, and not his actions; Ison and his jokes which were good; Mings always chewing tobacco and saying that it was what he lived on; Borkowski and his New Haven; Senft, Carrauthers, and Paegler; Sgt. Dudley and Sgt. Davies always wrestling; Sgt. Nichols and Sgt. Gribes always making us do what we were supposed to do; and all the rest, soon to slip out of the picture. It was really a good bunch.

On December 15, I stood guard outside our hut from 2300-2400. Official documents say that it was a cloudy night. I have to admit that I don't remember the weather conditions other than "for once" it was not snowing or raining. It was, rather, really a beautiful night, with the snow on the trees and ground, and all so quiet and peaceful. It was just as someone had said, "Who can expect anyone to fight in all this snow and cold. We'll be here all winter."

I went to sleep a little after midnight. Then, all of a sudden I woke up to a wham, bang, boom, crash. It sounded worse than the worst thunderstorm I'd ever been in. It was 5:30 in the morning, and artillery and mortar shells were hitting the trees and ground in the forest all around us. Boy what a noise and what a place to be in—in a sleeping bag, behind a few inches of fir logs. "Lord help us, because it is too late to move now." The history of the 394th says: "At 0530 on December 16, 1944, the 'great hour' struck. For almost two hours, a saturating barrage of all caliber of mortars, artillery, and multi-barreled rocket projectiles plastered the entire regimental front. Men who had been through North Africa, Sicily, and Normandy said it was the heaviest they had ever experienced."

**It was the beginning of Hitler's Ardennes offensive.**

Later we found that the focus of the German plan rested on their pushing right through our area, which was part of a wide series of valleys called the Losheim Gap. A small border crossing at Losheimergraben (See Map 1) would open the gate to the west. And that was right where we of A and B Company of the 394th were. Of course at the time we did not realize this. We just knew we had been badly shelled. What I remember was my reaction to the shelling. I shook and got jumpy as everything. Then I got so cold I thought that I was slowly becoming a chunk of ice. My heart raced like a steam engine, and I did not know what to do. "Should I get out of this sleeping bag and get into a foxhole or just stay where I am. If I make a run for a hole, I might get hit by shrapnel from a bursting shell. I am damned if I stay where I am, and I'm damned if I make a run for a fox-hole. I think I'll just stay here where I am and hope for the best." Finally about 7:00 the shelling stopped. I got up, put my shoes on, and put some coal on the fire. I tried to think of what I should do but found I just could not think. For the first time I realized one reason an attack is preceded by an artillery barrage. Shells were not just to kill people but to make soldiers unable to think what they should do.

Then Sgt. Frank, our first sergeant, came around and told everyone to fall out with rifles and belts. We were to take up a perimeter defense around the two-block area in which we had built our huts. It was a largely open area, with a few fairly good-sized fir trees here and there, with our huts among them. I soon found myself in a ditch by the road that ran from west to east into Germany. Mings was behind me and to the side behind a mound where he felt he was better protected. Across the road from us was a forested area. Forests in

Europe are usually planted. So the trees are all in a straight line. This was the case here, with the trees, therefore, all the same age. At this point the trees were from 15 to 20 feet high and so close together that someone could walk on the other side from us behind the first row of trees and could not be seen. This was the situation across the two-lane road to our north. On the east side of us was also a planted area with the trees also about the same height, and just as thick.

We had not been in our positions long when Mings and I saw soldiers, a column on each side of the road, coming up the road. They were so far away we did not shoot. But suddenly someone did shoot, and within a wink of the eye no one was to be seen. I waited, hunkered down in the ditch, looking down the road. Suddenly I was conscious of movement across the road from me. A German soldier stepped out and pulled up his burp gun (machine pistol) to shoot me. I can still see his face contorted with hate, looking at me as he raised his gun, positive he had me. My rifle was pointed down the road, so I would have to traverse my rifle a full 90 degrees, while all he had to do was just pull up his gun. I dropped to the bottom of the ditch, and bullets flew over me. A shot rang out from our side. Mings, in a most plaintive voice cried out, "Mac, you okay?" I said, "Yes." He said, "I don't think you are in a good position. Come over and join me." Well, I thought I was in a pretty good position, but I was all of a sudden feeling mighty lonely. So I came over to where he was and said, "Thanks." He said, "HEY, MAC, YOU KNOW WHAT? THIS IS SERIOUS BUSINESS. A GUY COULD GET KILLED."

Suddenly we heard blood-curdling screams from the

forest to our east. It sounded like one of our men had been caught in the area and was being tortured. But then we noticed that it had a scratchy sound to it. Someone yelled, "It's a recording." And I believe it was, for suddenly several enemy soldiers appeared at the edge of the woods and were immediately shot down.

And then the waiting set in. We could hear the sound of trucks, tanks, etc. moving on the roads at some distance from us and obviously going by us. We really did not know what was happening but sensed it was something awfully big. Finally one of our officers felt we had to make ourselves more space, especially if we had to stay in our position overnight. So he had us advance through the woods to our east, the woods so closely growing together that we could not see what was taking place in the next row of trees beyond us. It was a nerve-wracking process of going through the woods, one row at a time and no more, lest one group get ahead of the other, lose contact, and in confusion shoot one another. So, it was stepping through a row of trees—fearing to meet a German soldier face-to-face. Then, finding no enemy soldier in that line of trees, but rather your buddies, wait for the hand signal from the officer and stepping through to the next row of trees—fearing again to meet a German soldier.

We finally got through the forested area, which was probably about one city block wide. We came out in an old forest area, where there were only a few very large fir trees, with branches only way up high. The ground was carpeted with grass. It was really very beautiful, like walking in a public park. We slowly advanced. Suddenly someone began to shoot at us. The lieutenant

## 90  William F. McMurdie

urged us on, telling us to push the enemy back to a railroad cut that lay to our front, and which we could barely see through the trees. We now were all running forward in bursts, and hitting the ground, and shooting, getting up and going forward, shooting, and so forth. Suddenly heavy fire came our way. We all hit the ground. But no one could tell where the shots were coming from.

I looked to my right and slightly forward. Ison was behind a tree, but even though he was right-handed, he was on the left side of the tree shooting to his left. Why, I do not know. I was in a low spot and fired straight ahead. I realized that the ditch I was in must have been for draining water from the area to the railroad cut. Suddenly I looked to my right and saw bullet after bullet hitting Ison, and Sgt. Davies trying to pull him behind the tree. It was the most tragic sight I have ever seen. I felt so helpless, and could see that Sgt. Davies was doing all he could to pull Ison to safety, but obviously in vain. I kept firing to the front and saw a German soldier suddenly run up the far side of the railroad cut. He disappeared before I could take a shot at him. Suddenly we were told to retreat back to the thick forest line from which we had just come. We did so, and for me, PFC Robert Ison still lies beside that tree in Germany, a husband and father who had indeed given his life so his children and the rest of us could live in freedom. And always the question, why him and not me? Surely it is by the grace of God alone that we live.

Major Rusiecki in his book, *THE KEY TO THE BULGE: The Battle for Losheimergraben,* gives the following description of the situation: "LTC (Lieutenant Colonel) Douglas continued to receive reports at the command post. Since the morning artillery barrage had destroyed all landline communication, Douglas could make only sporadic contact with his companies via radio. The battalion commander was dismayed to see the new copper wire outside his CP (Command Post) torn and shredded. The Battalion Communications Platoon had expended a lot of effort to lay that wire. It was late morning. The first German attacks from the south and east were several hours old. Companies A and B took the brunt of the German attacks, with Company B losing 60 percent of its troops in a few hours. . . . Company A took many casualties as well, perhaps 30 percent of its total strength. Company A still held its original position. . . . but LTC Douglas still did not have a clear grasp of the big picture. . . ." (p.56)

That night we took up a defense around the city block area thick with trees. Of course we had no food, and had had none all day. We had water, but I could not tell you where from. We were completely separated from the rest of our division, and really did not know what was what.

We spent one miserable night. We took turns on guard duty, which meant getting into a half-ton truck that we had found and backing it into the woods in the middle of the line. And what a night. We already were exhausted from the events of the day. As we took turns being on guard, we did not do a good job of it. The idea was to blow the horn if the enemy came upon us. Several times the horn blew. We all woke up, fearing the worst. We would hear, "Sorry!!!" The person on guard had become sleepy and fallen onto the horn.

The next day was spent guarding the ground we held, and wondering what was happening. We sensed that a mighty big battle was in progress, for we could still hear vehicles going by on the nearby roads and also big guns firing almost constantly. The officers informed us that we were going to hold where we were for the day, and if we did not hear otherwise, at dusk, would head for our lines. We could tell, in general, where the main battle was raging and where our lines were since we could recognize the sound of our artillery.

While some of us did not see much action that second day, something was happening to an assortment of soldiers which included men from our A Company. What happened was this: Our men held the custom houses near Losheimergraben and defended them against the attacking Germans under Oberstleutnant Osterhold. In time, Osterhold's men completely surrounded the houses and planned on sneaking up to them and throwing high explosives through the basement windows and killing all our men. Osterhold himself led the sneak attack. Rusiecki recounts what happened:

"As he prepared to pull the fuse and throw the mine, Osterhold stopped. He realized that the mine would create a terrific explosion within the enclosed space of the house. The young men inside would suffer a horrible, senseless death. Somewhat fluent in English, Osterhold mustered every word he knew and called to the Americans in the houses: 'Hello there! Can you hear me?' He heard some faint responses like 'Go to hell, kraut' and a couple of other comments. Osterhold was now aware they could hear him. He called again, 'I am the commander of this infantry unit. We've already encircled you. There's no reason to continue this struggle. You have fought honorably and we recognize this. We're not SS soldiers and we will not harm you. If you surrender, I'll personally guarantee that your personal possessions will remain with you. If you don't surrender, I will be forced to throw some quick-fuse mines into the houses and kill all of you.'"

Rusiecki then tells how Osterhold talked over surrender terms with the men commanding our Army unit and how he spoke to his own troops, calling upon them not to fire as the men came out of the buildings. He then went into one of the buildings and found 40 men in this one building alone. But as they talked things over he realized that something was wrong. "What's the matter?" Osterhold asked. Several young soldiers produced hand grenades from behind their backs and showed them to Osterhold. "We can't find the pins," said one of them. Another recommended tossing the grenades out the window and letting them explode. "No!" cried Osterhold. "I have no way of telling my men outside what is happening. This act might revive the battle. My soldiers might think you ambushed me." Osterhold produced a flashlight and everyone, including Osterhold, got down on his hands and knees to look for the pins. One by one they found the pins and placed them back into the grenades. Osterhold and the Americans emerged from the basement and into the waiting arms of the German grenadiers. . . . Osterhold was astounded to see that the prisoners from all the houses numbered nearly one hundred." It is interesting that later on our own 99th Infantrymen liberated some of these captured men of the 99th from the POW camp where they were held. (pp.143-144)

Returning to my situation on that second day of the Battle of the Bulge, all of us tried to find something to eat but found nothing. About 4:00 in the afternoon, the officers said we would make a brief attack north to clear the woods in case some Jerries were observing us. We did not want them to see us leave the area at dusk. We had all felt that someone was in the wooded area north of us observing us and waiting until they could easily take us. So it was that we walked single file east on the road, parallel to the woods we actually wanted to clear. Then about a block from where we had started, still in single file, we turned north and went about 10 paces and then turned, still in a single column, and walked into the woods between two rows of the tightly growing trees. The idea was to form a line of men that would then sweep left, en masse, to the road, thus clearing the area. Of course, we all hoped no one would actually be in this small area of woods. Suddenly not far in front of me were several German soldiers, obviously working at making supper. They had a little fire going in a clearing about 100 feet in front of us. I put up my hand to stop the fellows behind me and pointed toward the German soldiers, very much worried that the Germans would see me before we were really ready to take them on. Several fellows moved up to my right and left.

A noise suddenly attracted the Germans. They grabbed for their rifles. I now believe what happened was that Al Haefner had gone to the right and was moving toward them, rather than standing with us since we were so closely crowded together because of the fir trees. His movement must have in some way alerted the German soldiers to our approach. But just as they looked up and grabbed their rifles and began to shoot, we all shot at them. They then turned (too late) to try to shoot us. Sad to say, I believe they did get Al, for we never saw him again. Then, almost at the same time, we were told to move toward our original position, since we were in the right place to make our move and clear the forest. Just as we made our move, a burp gun opened up to our left. The bullets trimmed the tree next to Mings, just as if you had cut them with a hedge trimmer. "Comrade! Comrade!" came a cry. The German who had done the shooting suddenly realized he was greatly outnumbered and so wanted to surrender. The guys said some very nasty words to the effect that he should have surrendered before and not shot at us, and then they shot him down. I know you will not like to read that this was done, but it was.

We all immediately crossed the road. As we did, we noticed a man lying near where we had left our area to clear the woods. It was Sgt. George Dorner. He had been the last man to leave the area and had been shot down by the Germans. I had been the first to leave the area and realized the German could have just as well shot me.

We all assembled immediately in the area opposite the area we had just cleared. It was dusk, and we formed a long line and followed our captain out of our area, toward where we could hear our guns firing. It got dark quickly as we walked along, fearing every moment that we would be discovered and shot down. I would guess that there were over 100 of us. Suddenly a German soldier cried out "Halt." We stood still for a short time, never saying a word, and then went on. I guess the

German soldier could not see who we really were, and since we were a large number, probably thought we were friendly troops. On we went through the night, stumbling and going through forested areas so dark we had to hang on to the man's belt in front of us to keep from being separated and lost. We went over stone walls. Once I almost stepped into a well, not at first seeing that the "wall" was circular, and actually a well. Then we went though a very wooded area and a group of about 20 of us found ourselves separated from the others. We did not know what to do so decided to go to sleep and try to figure things out the next morning. We were in such a wooded area that we felt we were not likely to be noticed.

Dawn found us in a very beautiful park-like wooded area. We wanted to find our own lines as quickly as possible. But we also wanted to find something to eat. We were starving, having eaten nothing for two days. We began to walk toward the sound of our artillery. We came across a field of turnips; that is, we thought they were turnips. We pulled some of them up, took our bayonets and cut them up and began to eat them. They were awful. Later we found that the reason they tasted so terrible was that they were not turnips, but sugar beets, which have an acid of some sort in them.

Throwing the sugar beets away, we went on and came across some abandoned U.S. Army vehicles. We looked through them and found some D-Bars. These were emergency food rations, and were absolutely delicious. With these in hand, and eating them as we went, we finally came to our lines. But remember, we were behind the German lines—the Germans facing our lines. So it was that we came up behind some German soldiers, who quickly surrendered to us. But then we had the problem of convincing our own troops who we were. We yelled and hollered and finally were accepted as soldiers who had made their way back to our own lines. We were then told to proceed toward the city of Elsenborn, Belgium, and were shown the way. Everyone was moving back as we went across the country. In front of Elsenborn we saw our 105 self-propelled guns. They were firing for all they were worth, and also preparing to depart at a moment's notice. We got to Elsenborn and a giant kitchen that the regiment had set up. We finally got all the food we wanted, and we were reunited with our outfit. Colonel Douglas, our Battalion Commander, almost cried when he saw us. So many men had been lost, and he felt personally responsible.

Lieutenant Colonel Robert H. Douglas, Commanding Officer 1st Battalion, 394th Infantry

The story of the 394th Infantry says, "Co. A's position was never penetrated despite repeated attacks upon it. Outflanked and hard-pressed, this company stood fast till just before dusk. Then it counter-attacked the enemy attempting to mop up Losheimergraben. After expending all its mortar ammo, Co. A, together with the few survivors of the bloody battle of the crossroads, withdrew with the 3rd Bn. under the cover of darkness through four miles of enemy-held territory to Murringen. On the 18th, the 1st and 3rd Battalions, together with medical and headquarters units, drew back to Elsenborn, Belgium, via Krinkelt and Wirtzfelt."

It surely was a sad sight to behold. Across the fields, down the roads, on jeeps and on foot, came soldiers from at least 5 different divisions. They were not organized in any way-just coming in by two's and three's, or maybe a group of 10 or 20 like us. We saw big Lieutenant Plankers of "C" Company leading in 8 men. He said, "We are "C" Company." (Remember, a company is about 180 men.) Each group was what had managed to escape being killed, captured, or wounded by Hitler's troops. It was rough, mighty rough. We had lost plenty, but we soon realized that our Company "A" had not been hit the worst. Everyone was feeling the same— terribly demoralized.

General Lauer's exact words from his book says, "We had gotten our unit back. The losses they had suffered were grievous. Companies of battalions which had sustained the brunt of the attack had been reduced to thirty or sixty men from 187. Battalions which had entered the fight with 825 men came back to organize Elsenborn

Ridge with a meager strength of 160 to 200 men. No accurate figures could be obtained at the time." (pp.68-69)

Rusiecki says of our 1st Battalion of 825 men and made up of A, B, C, and D companies: "Only 260 officers and men from the original unit made it out of Losheimergraben. LTC Douglas still commanded the battalion and would do so until the final victory in Germany." (p.149) And, I might as well say here that I remember talking to LTC Douglas several times and was always well impressed with him as our Battalion Commander.

Returning to the situation in Elsenborn, we were finally put in a barn to get some sleep. This "barn" was very unique. Downstairs were the living room, dining room, bedrooms, kitchen, etc., plus stalls for the cows. The hay barn was then above all of this. It seemed such an odd arrangement until it dawned on us that the body heat from the cows was actually keeping the whole area warm.

*Major General Walter Lauer, Commanding General, 99th Infantry Division. From* DAUNTLESS/ *John Rogers, Jr.* 393 HQ

In the morning we got up, ate, and then everyone wanted to know what we were going to do. We felt we had fought so hard and gloriously that we should have at least a few days off. We were soon disabused of that idea. We were told just what the Germans were doing and that the battle was far from over. If the Germans were able to make it to Antwerp and cut us off, we would be in big trouble and the whole war would be changed, not in our favor. Immediately we were to be put into the front lines as a defense against any possible attack in our area.

Sgt. Davies told me that I was now assistant squad leader. Boyles was not returning from sick call. Two guys had been killed, including Ison. Scartz had been at rest camp, which we heard had been captured. There were only 8 of the 12 of us left. After lunch came the order to pack up and move out. We walked about 3 miles out of Elsenborn toward Rockerath to what is known as Elsenborn Ridge. (See Map 2)

At dusk our squad began to dig in about 100 yards from 13 trees that pointed toward the enemy and stood alone on an otherwise open piece of farmland. We were about 75 yards down the reverse slope of high ground. The area gradually sloped down toward the unseen Germans who must have been a 1000 yards in front of us. Sgt. Davies and I took turns digging and sleeping. The ground was frozen. We would sleep as long as we could, and when the cold awakened us, we took our turn digging and got a little warmed up again from the work. With our entrenching tools (little shovels), which were pointed, we could only chip out little pieces at a time. Sgt. Davies would check our line of guys every once in a while. We were digging holes about 50 feet or so apart—digging as if our lives depended on it. And they did, for we were told that we were not to move from our positions unless it was to go forward. We got down about 18 inches through the frozen ground before we got to regular earth and could dig at a decent rate. At this time another fellow and I went out where the trees were and ripped down a shack that was there.

Our fox holes were in the shape of an L. The longer part of the L was about 7 feet long (since I am 6 feet 4 inches tall). The other part about 5 feet long. We took the timbers from the shack and the wood from the sides, put it all across the long part of our hole, and then put all of the dirt on top of the wood, or behind us. We put a blanket across the entrance to the covered area, where we would then sleep. We stood in the other area, kept an eye on the enemy, and made it as good a defensive position as we could, especially by putting dirt behind us and slightly above head height. Thus our helmeted heads would blend in with the background. Of course, we took turns in the fighting part of the hole, day and night. Otherwise we slept or did whatever we needed to do in order to keep alive and in fighting shape.

On December 19 artillery moved in several city blocks behind us. An artillery man came to Sgt. Davies and asked if we would be artillery spotters. He explained that they were short of men and would show us what to do. Sgt. Davies gave me the job, and so I listened as the artillery man gave me a voice phone and walked me through what I was supposed to do. Basically all I was to do was tell the men by phone where the shells were landing so they could adjust their guns, and in the end hit their targets. Of course, they were in a big hurry because we all knew we might be attacked at any time.

Soon I heard a whistle in the phone, the signal to pick it up and talk to the artillery fellows. The gunner explained that they were going to fire one round. I was to see where it landed so they could zero in their guns. They fired. I can still see and feel what happened. The shell landed about 3 feet in front of my position. If I had not been standing in the fox hole with my head barely above the ground, I surely would have been hit, and really don't know why I wasn't hit. The gunner asked where the shell had landed. I told him, "I am picking hot metal out of the hole in front of me; that is where it landed." His only reply was, "Sorry." I then asked that he please "up" his elevation. He said they would, and then told me that another round was coming. It landed to my left. Two machine gunners disappeared. We never found enough of them to have something to bury. I was very upset, and very angry, and very disgusted. When I explained to the gunner what had happened he again said, "Sorry, but." "Yes, but what?" I asked. I have always felt that they had been in such a hurry they did not dig in their gun properly, and thus were the cause of the death of two good soldiers. But being killed by friendly fire is something that happens in a war whether one likes to admit it or not. (In the Civil War, Stonewall Jackson was fatally wounded by one of his own soldiers.) They fired another round which landed well forward of our position. With a few more rounds, they had their guns sighted in.

About then Sgt. Gribes came and said that Paris had gone a little "buggy" over what had happened to the two machine gunners. He had had to send him back.

As night fell on December 20, we could hear engines

being fired up in front of us. Then we thought we could hear tanks moving forward in great numbers. We knew we were done for if they ever got to us, since we had nothing with which to fight tanks. Then we came under artillery bombardment. We really could not see anything for sure. We made contact with our artillery by means of the phone. They informed us that they would soon be firing. And they did. The shells fell in front of us, and then were advanced toward the enemy like marching troops. It was awesome—the shells bursting and advancing toward the enemy. In the morning we looked out and saw 3 German tanks, a bulldozer, and some half-tracks, all in ruins. In the official history of the 394th Infantry it says, "Dec. 20, 1944. . . . Jerries throw tank and infantry attack at 1st Bn., are stopped cold by artillery." (1st Battalion was made up of A, B, C, and D companies. We were company A.) (See Map. 2)

The next day several fellows went on sick call, and we later heard that their trouble was that they had trench foot. This happens when you do not take proper care of your feet. Already you have probably noted that our boots were not really what we needed for the situation we were in. They did not keep our feet warm enough, and they let in water. We were supposed to take off our boots every day and examine our feet and make sure they were okay and then put on new, clean, dry socks. Some of the guys felt okay, so had neglected to do this. Now they were taking off their boots to put on clean, dry, socks, only to find that their feet had turned black. Reason: trench foot, a lack of circulation which can end up in gangrene, requiring the amputation of your foot. So back the men went. Later we heard that some were in England being treated. Some, including Mings, returned to us in a few weeks.

Sgt. Davies was one of those who was sent back, never to return. Sgt. Dudley of the 2nd squad came over to be with me. His feet were giving him trouble so he did not wear boots. But he was wearing 7 pairs of socks worn in overshoes that they had just given us. I was having trouble with keeping my feet warm and dry. My solution was to cut the front part of my boots out, just in front of the place where the shoe laces begin, and wear several pairs of socks, and wear this combination inside my water proof overshoes. This worked for me.

The Germans now began to keep us on our toes by putting a few mortar shells into our position, or taking pot shots at us when we went back to meet nature's needs, or to get food or other supplies. Of course we looked closely at where we believed they were holed up before we would get out of our holes. But you could rarely see them since they were in a wooded area, while on the other hand we were out in the open.

Sgt. Dudley thought our hole was not good enough, so he took all the dirt off the timbers, dug our hole a little deeper and wider, put the timbers and dirt all back, and put little bushes he had found on top of the dirt. It really was a masterful bit of camouflage. It was more comfortable, including his addition of a lamp inside our sleeping area. Our lamp was a water canteen filled with gasoline, with a sock as a wick. This we kept burning inside our sleeping area. It gave a little light in an otherwise dark spot, and also a little heat. Of course it was not really a good idea, since we made no provision for air to get in and carbon monoxide and soot to get out. What it did in time to all the exposed parts of our bodies you can imagine. At this time we also were determined to make our "bed" dry. So we began collecting all the blankets we could and then laid them down on the ground where we slept, which of course was about 6 feet below ground level. I remember that at the 16th blanket, properly folded and put in place, we decided we were "dry." Below that, the blankets were more and more damp. And of course we always slept with all our clothes on. In fact it would be over a month before we were in a position to get cleaned up and have a change of clothes. You might wonder where we got all of the blankets. When you consider all the men going back on sick call and never returning because of having trench foot, you realize we had lots of spare stuff.

Our position was at the corner of the Bulge. (See Map 2) Writing about this in July of 1945, I said, "We were at the corner where the line turned from going south to west. We had the corner, and it was very important that we keep it because we were on high ground just in front of Elsenborn which was the supply and transportation center for 4 Divisions: the 9th on our left, the 2nd on our right, the 1st to the right of that, and us, the 99th. Elsenborn was also the supply center for artillery and tank units in the neighborhood."

I did not realize, at the time, the importance of our efforts that stopped Hitler's armies. But Dick Byers, a fellow 99th Division soldier, sent me a quote that shows how important our resistance was. The quote is from the MILITARY HISTORY QUARTERLY: Vol. 3. No. I, 1989. The author of this article on the Battle of the Bulge is Prof. Stephen Ambrose who has now become famous as the author of the book, *CITIZEN SOLDIERS*.

In part Ambrose writes:

> "The U.S. 99th Infantry Division, newly arrived in Europe, and the 2nd Infantry Division, which had come ashore at Utah Beach . . . did not simply delay the German advances but stopped it along the critical point of the whole battle, Elsenborn Ridge. This low ridge lay across the direct line from the Eifel to Antwerp and was the main objective of Sepp Dietrich's Sixth Panzer Army."

> "Elsenborn Ridge was the Little Round Top of the battle. Dietrich drove his units mercilessly, but he could not take it. In the vast literature on the Battle of the Bulge, Elsenborn Ridge always yields pride of place to the far more famous action to the south, at Bastogne. Everyone knows about the 101st Airborne at Bastogne; almost no one knows even the names of the Ninety-ninth and the Second infantries. Yet it was was along the Elsenborn Ridge, on the first and second day, that these two ordinary infantry divisions, largely out of touch with their commands, outnumbered five to one and worse, outgunned and surprised, managed to stop the Germans in their main line of advance. The Germans never did take the ridge.

> "The practical effect of the Elsenborn resistance was . . . that the offensive no longer had a strategic objective. Von Runstedt, and even Dietrich, recognized this immediately. . . on December 17th.

"Thus did a bunch of junior officers, noncoms, and privates, many of them new to battle, some of them exhausted by six months of continuous warfare, prove that Hitler was wrong to think that the American GI could not fight."

About noon one day a German came out and started to tinker with an abandoned Jeep of ours that was about 750 feet to our front and about 250 yards from the German lines. It had snowed so he first dug the snow away. We didn't think much of it, since we did not think the Jeep would run even if he managed to try it. Guys took a few shots at him, but they all missed. With field glasses we then saw that he was working on the Jeep. The artillery guys sent a few rounds his way, but he still kept working on the Jeep. It took him 2 hours but he finally got the Jeep running and drove off. We were very surprised and disgusted that we had not stopped him from getting away with "our" Jeep.

About December 23 they decided it was necessary for each platoon to operate an outpost. So a group went out to dig it. An engineer was kind enough to come and blow us a hole to get us started. It took about 3 hours for 3 guys to dig the round hole into a square and make it into an outpost. We used the remainder of the shack for a roof, threw dirt over it and snow over that, and an opening was left to get in and out and for observation. We stayed out for the first night. The night was clear, so it wasn't bad, but even at that you could not help but imagine that guys were sneaking up on you. It was very nerve-wracking.

December 24 came. I remember that night, because just after dark I was standing guard and felt so lonesome I almost cried. I could see my Mom and Dad, sister Jean, and brother Jack getting into our car and going to church for our usual Christmas Eve children's service. I could just see the car going down Brigden Road and turn down Allen Ave. to the church which was on the corner of the street just below Brigden. I could see the kids recite the different parts of the Christmas story, and hear them sing *Hark the Herald Angels Sing, Silent Night, Holy Night,* etc. And why should I have to be in this God-forsaken place in Germany, perhaps to be killed. But then I told myself that my dad was too old to fight, and my brother too young, and that left me to do a job that just needed to be done. But it did not mean that I needed to like it, which I certainly did not.

I wrote a letter home on December 27. In it I mention the Battle of the Bulge in brief, but then also say:
**"On Christmas Day I got 2 packages, one from the Lakes, the other from Mrs. Fecht. The Lakes sent me canned grapefruit juice, olives, and candy. The Fechts sent a box of their swell candy and this stationery that I've wanted for so long. We had a swell dinner - turkey and all on Christmas Day. It tasted sort of funny after a week of C and K rations. . . . I've found out one thing, and that is that you don't need much to exist on. We did all right with the little we had. I'm hoping that the Jerries didn't capture any of your packages to me. They got lots of them, I'm afraid. I sure was glad to get the 2 packages I did."**

General Lauer also sent us all a Christmas letter:

*CHIDSTMAS GREETINGS
to
EACH AND EVERY SOLDIER OF THE 99TH*

*It is with the greatest pride that I greet the heroic soldiers, and the title of soldier applies to officers who are proud to call themselves soldiers, on this turbulent approaching Christmas time. The individual and collective fighting of the gallant 99th has been superb. It can be described only in superlative praise. Although this Christmas may be troublesome and not in keeping with our best traditions, it will be a sacrifice to the brilliant, happy and peaceful Christmases that will be celebrated in years to come.*

*May God bless you, merry gentlemen, and let nothing you dismay.*

On the days after Christmas, our Air Force was out in full force. In 1945, I wrote:

**"For a while we wondered if our Air Force was all destroyed, because the Germans would strike Elsenborn and bomb away without anything but ack-ack shooting back. Around Christmas our boys really came out in full though. From then on when we looked up we only saw stars, not black crosses. It sure was a beautiful sight to see thousands of planes flying over with the vapor trails marking where they had gone. We sure enjoyed those clear cold days when the Air Corps came over. We knew that the**

**war was beginning to go our way."**

In "The Story of the 394th Infantry" it says the following: "Dec. 28, 1944. . . . Nazis try again, using 2 battalions of infantry and 10 S-P guns, to pierce 1st Bn. lines, are slaughtered by small arms, mortar, and artillery." (What is meant is that the Nazis were making another attempt to encircle our armies and destroy or capture us.)

For Sgt. Dudley and me this is what happened. Long and Meehan came running back from the outpost yelling, "It is the Jerries, they are coming." It was pitch black, about 5:30 a.m. Suddenly all we could see were tracers going over our head, and we heard artillery shells landing all around us, along with the sound of German machine guns. Their machine guns fired so rapidly that it sounded like someone tearing a bed sheet. But then we could hear what we thought were the sounds of men crawling toward us. We recklessly shot into the blackness, threw a few hand grenades also, and were so nervous at first that we were in danger of using up all our ammunition. Then for a while it was very, very quiet. We realized we had to stop shooting into the darkness and make our efforts mean something. We felt sure men were crawling toward us, so once or twice we threw grenades out, hoping they would discourage anyone from coming our way. Then "for sure" we heard movement. We had our voice phone, so we called for flares to be shot in front of us to give light to the situation. The flares went off, and we saw men moving toward us, and a few even running by us to our right. Of course we now had something to shoot at. We told the mortar men to keep it up and add other stuff. They did.

Dudley began praying like everything. We both thought that we were done for. He admitted doing all kinds of bad things. I knew he was no angel, but what he asked God to forgive him for, was news to me. He suddenly stopped praying and said, "Mac, I've never prayed before in my life. I wonder if it will do any good." Well, he wasn't the only one who was praying.

The battle suddenly went quiet again, and we wondered what was going to happen next. It worried us that we had seen German soldiers run by to our right. Slowly it became light. In the light we realized that there were enemy soldiers in the fox hole to our right, and so we shot a few shots that way. Then we noticed they were waving a white flag, so we stopped shooting at them. But we kept waiting for more light, not really knowing what to do. Finally we yelled at them to come out. Two of them did. Then here and there others began getting up, till we counted 6 more of them. Later we found two dead, and one very badly wounded. He died later. Behind our hole and to the right, lay another. One of the lieutenants, I think it was Lt. Gullette, came forward, so we very carefully got out of our hole, and with him looked over the situation.

Two of the Germans were wounded. An older German soldier had surrendered, and he spoke English. He looked to be in his 60s and acted very much the professional soldier. He had been the leader. One German soldier turned out to be a youth of perhaps 15 or 16. When we came up to them the old gentleman was standing, as were a few others, but the boy was crouched down. We took it that he had surrendered, when suddenly he pulled out a gun, and at such close range began shooting at us. His face was contorted with a look of pure hate and defiance. We really had no time to think, but just stood there in amazement that at this moment someone would start shooting. Why none of us were hit, I don't know. One of our fellows, I don't remember who, had a .45 pistol in his hand and shot the kid dead with one shot. The German officer shook his head and said, "Hitler Jugen (Youth), what a waste, what a waste." He was speaking of the young people who were trained by Hitler in his way of thinking. This officer was from the regular German Army, while the youth had been part of the Nazi movement. And we had already noticed that the regular German Army guys were really decent people, doing their job as loyal Germans. The SS troopers and "Hitler Youth" on the other hand were fanatical, and were filled with an anger and a hate that was so foreign to anything that we had ever experienced.

We then began looking over the area very carefully to make sure we could account for all who had been in on the attack. As we looked about we saw that some of the Germans were as close to our holes as 10 yards. By night we had all of the dead picked up. We didn't want them around. I found one, dug in, but shot right through the head about 100 yards away from us. He had been killed by luck because no one saw him until I discovered him just about dark. He had probably been killed by machine gun fire since our machine gunners had shot up the whole area several times. What seems a wonder is that any of the German soldiers had come through alive.

Toward the end of rounding the Germans up, and just before we sent them back, a very strange thing happened. At least it has always seemed strange to me.

We offered cigarettes to them. They gladly accepted them. We treated them with great respect, just as if we had just ended a nice ball game, and since the game was over, it was time to take a break. They offered us what they had, which was some very coarse dark brown bread, and something in a tin that turned out to be lard. They used it just like we use butter. I could not help but wonder how people could live on such food, but evidently they did. The most interesting thing they came up with were canned sardines from Portugal. I thought that was interesting. By the way, in this whole encounter we had not lost any men, but a few were wounded.

Next day Dudley went back to the Aid Station. He had aches and pains all over, and his feet were not in good shape. I did not know it at the time but found out later that these were the signs of trench foot. Pageler came up to be with me. The rest of the fellows—Mings, Senft, Seagraves, and others—had also gone back. Of the 39 of us who had started in the Battle of the Bulge, only 4 of us were now left: Sgt. Nichols, Paegler, Meehan and me. Our holes at first were filled by C Company and the outpost was run by us with 2nd Battalion men from G company. But slowly our ranks were filled with replacements from the States and from the air fields of England. We wondered if these men would really work out as front line Infantry soldiers.

I remember having to place a group of them in our holes. This was done at night so the Germans would not know what was happening. I would take a man to a hole, tell him the password for the evening, and then point in the direction of the enemy. Of course, they were terribly confused having never seen any of our area in the day time. Finally I put a guy by the name of Bishop in place. I carefully told him the direction of the enemy. I also told him that I would be back later to check on things and make sure everything was okay.

After I had placed everyone, I went back to make my check. I carefully came up behind the men, and made sure they knew I was coming. Finally I came up to Bishop. He yelled, "Halt, who goes there." He had heard me, and said the right thing, but it seemed to me that he was facing the wrong way, me, rather than the enemy. I gave him the password, and with his permission came up to him. Sure enough, he was facing me, and had his back to the enemy. I pointed this out to him. He insisted that he was facing the right way. I had an awful time convincing him that I surely knew more about the situation than he.

January 1944 was one of the coldest in history. At least so say the history books. General Lauer describes the month: "For the men of the 99th Division, most of the month of January was one of licking its wounds, repairing the damage done, re-equipping, receiving replacements, holding the front assigned on the 'Hot Corner,' conducting patrols into the enemy's lines, staging demonstrations against the enemy, and trying to make life as bearable as possible on open, wind-swept Elsenborn Ridge."

For me January was one hellish story. For example, if it snowed much we would have to clean the packed down snow out of the hole. It got packed down because when we stood guard we would step back and forth in the hole and thus pack it down. One could not throw it out as it came down. Then there was going back for supplies and being shot at. The bullet would go by (hopefully) and if it was close it sounded like someone snapping his fingers right by your ear. If it was farther away, you could still hear a little "snap," and then the boom from the German side. Then there was mortar fire. The Germans really knew how to use their mortars, so you had to be alert at all times for them. What you heard was a click, click, click sound from their side. Then you knew you had about 10 seconds to do whatever you wished. (A mortar shell travels in a high circular arc. An artillery shell travels almost parallel to the ground.) I always counted to 10 slowly and then hit the dirt. They usually missed. But not always.

We had a fellow we called Wooton. What his real name was I can't remember. He, like Mings, was from Kentucky. But he could not seem to focus on the fact that he was on the front and had to keep alert. He always seemed to be in a daze. One day it was his turn to go back and pick up the rations and deliver some to each of us. I heard the click, click, click and knew mortar shells were on their way. So I looked around to see if anyone was walking about. Sure enough, there was Wooton bringing us our rations and walking along as if he was walking home from the store. He was quite a ways away from me, but I yelled as loud as I could for him to hit the dirt. But he didn't hear me, and the mortar shell lit right in front of him. It killed him instantly. Later, when the K rations he had been bringing up were brought to me, I could not eat them.

Another time I was checking the holes. I did this daily to make sure the guys were okay. I would also give them socks, or whatever else they needed, including some things they did not need but the government kept sending up, namely cigarettes and cigars. I was walking along in a straight line from my hole to the next one when I heard the click, click, click. I went along, counting to ten and hit the dirt. The first mortar shell landed 100 feet behind me; the next lit 50 feet behind me. I realized the next was going to land right on me. I wondered, should I roll to the right, or the left. Of course all of these thoughts came in a split second. I actually rolled to the right, but then rolled back to where I started. The shell landed to the right of me. It cut up the elbow section of my field jacket and peppered me with unburned powder. The noise of the explosion made my ears ring. I can only record that my reaction was slightly irrational. I lay there for a while and then went back to our company commander and told him what had happened. But I carried on as if I were half nuts. I know that later I felt odd about acting in such a fashion. I can only say that I was thankful to God to be alive. One thing you realized more and more in combat is that to keep alive, you just have to be alert at all times. But you also realized that this alone is not enough. The dear Lord has to keep you in His protective care, or you will just not make it.

And this was something that I thought about quite a bit. Could I expect God to keep me alive, just because I believed that He had sent His Son as the promised Messiah and Savior of the world? Thinking about what I knew about the teachings of the Bible, I realized I could not necessarily expect to come out alive. But I did come to where I was confident that the Lord would care for me, and even if I did die, He would take me to be with Him in heaven. And this, not on the basis of anything I had done, but what Jesus had done for me. This gave me a certain sense of well-being that I cannot really explain. Also, one prayer of mine was the same as many others, "Lord, just don't let me get shot up so that I am a cripple for the rest of my life."

In a letter dated January 6, 1945, I mentioned receiving letters from my folks and then saying:

**"At the time of your letter we weren't near where you said. I'm not exactly sure what I can say, but we are somewhere on the line in front of Verviers. - I can stand a package with some canned milk, preserves of any sort, and maybe some dried fruit or cookies. I wish I were home too, more than you can ever imagine. I'm still getting along, and still hoping and praying for the end of this war. They called up just now and said I'm a Buck Sergeant officially. Just means a little more work I'm afraid, but someone has to do it."**

As before said, our replacements were mostly men not trained for the infantry. We did our best to instruct them and to make sure they kept their weapons clean and their socks changed, etc. The biggest challenge for them seemed to be to take their turn at outpost duty. I did not blame them, since it was really scary to be out there, even if you were there with one or two others. You were out front, and if attacked, you were the most vulnerable. One evening Bishop was out there with some other fellows. They had gone out just before dark

About 6 or 7 in the evening, I got a call from Bishop, "Sarge, something is coming toward me. What do I do?" I looked out toward the enemy lines and could see absolutely nothing unusual, and told him so. I said, "Just keep alert, you're okay." Hardly any time went by and he called on the phone again. "Sarge, I think the Germans have some secret weapon. It's coming right toward us. You have to let me come back." I looked out toward the enemy lines again. I could see absolutely nothing unusual. I told him, "You get out of that hole and come back, and I'll take a shot at you. I don't see a thing." He was really upsetting me. There was absolutely nothing out there that was out of the ordinary. A little time went by and he called again. He pleaded with me to let him come back I looked, but again saw nothing out of place. He pleaded with me to call the Lieutenant. I said, "Okay, but he probably has gone to bed and will not like this." "Please," came back the plaintive cry.

I called Lt. Gullette. I explained what had happened. He could have refused to do anything. But he was a wonderful officer and very thoughtful of the troops. He understood what it was like being on outpost. He said he would take a look. Bishop, of course, was on the line and heard him say this. Finally, the Lieutenant came back. He said, "All I see is the moon rising." "Oh," we heard Bishop say, "The moon." Yes, that is all it was; but as the full moon slowly rose, and got larger and larger, he thought it was some fiery new weapon the Germans had invented.

It is hard to know what to include in this account of my war experiences. But January of 1945 was one day after another of very routine things, with some variations. Several things come to mind. Our rations were all K rations. We were supposed to eat one for each meal, but most of us were eating 5 or 6 a day. These rations came in cracker-jack-sized paraffin boxes. They would each have a can in them the size of a tuna can. The can might be of cheese, ham and eggs, stew, or spaghetti and meatballs.  Besides this would be some biscuits, a package of powdered coffee or cocoa, some candy and toilet paper.  To make coffee or cocoa we would take water, put it in our canteen, and heat it by burning the paraffin package or by heating it over our canteen that had the gasoline in it.  We would then pour in the coffee or cocoa mix.  It really tasted fairly good.  Once in a while they would send up a loaf of bread.  We would dip pieces of bread into our cocoa mix, and that was a real treat.

Every day we each had to go back and get water and gasoline.  The gasoline was for our "lamps" that gave us both light and a little heat.  Both were in canteens meant for water, and one needed to be careful not to mix up the two.  One day I did forget and took a good swig of gasoline.  A small amount went down, but most of it I spit out as quickly as I could.  No harm ever came from it all, but it made for a very nasty experience.

We tried to warm some water each day and shave and wash our hands and faces.  But this was not done as often as we should have done it.  We also had to take off our shoes and put on new socks.  This was a must.  No excuses.  Then there was cleaning our weapon every day, especially since the M-1 did not work well unless almost perfectly clean.

That was especially brought home after the battle of December 28.  Afterwards, I went up to the men in the hole just to my left.  Getting there I saw a dead German not 10 feet in front of them.  I asked how it was possible that a German soldier had gotten so close.  They said they did not know.  I asked to see their rifles.  The guys were always giving me trouble about cleaning them. I took the rifles one by one, and worked the mechanism, and every gun was sticky. I said to them, "Your rifles were not firing properly, were they?" They admitted this was the case and that they had not been able to get them to fire after the first round or two because they jammed.

Another job was repairing communications lines. The Germans regularly lobbed mortar shells at us, as previously mentioned. These sometimes would cut our only communications line which was our voice phone. This meant someone had to follow the line and find the break and fix it. Then there were patrols.

It was on the 18th of January when I was told that a big patrol was going out that night to pick up German prisoners in order to question them and get information about what the Germans opposite us were doing. I was told I would be the Sgt. in reserve in case anything happened to one of the other fellows. Sgt. Carl Boehme was to be the leader, and another fellow I did not know his assistant. He had helped layout a mine field in front of the area through which they would have to go to get to the enemy. So he would guide them. Just after dark they started off in a snowstorm. Going through the mine field, the man who had laid them stepped on one of the very mines he had laid and was badly injured. It was snowing so hard he had taken a wrong turn. They came back to the command post with their casualty and sent for me. I really did not want to go, for of all things, it was not only snowing but snowing hard. But the Colonel said, "You go." I went.

Boehme led off. There were 12 of us in all. In the

middle we had a radio man. I brought up the rear. It was snowing so hard we had to keep very close to each other or get lost, and none of us wanted to get lost in a snowstorm. Boehme was following a compass reading to get to the German lines. Remember, we were out in the open, the Germans were in the woods. We had long ago noted that they had built shelters of some sort just behind the front line of trees. So our plan was to hit the trees, go in one row, and go along until we found some Germans. It seemed forever before we hit the tree line. But we finally did. Boehme went in and turned right, and after a while came to a hut-like structure. He stuck his rifle in and flipped back the blanket being used for a door. They were playing cards by candlelight. He told them to keep quiet and come with us or they would be two dead Germans. They came. We immediately went back the way we had come, in single file. Sergeant Boehme went first, then a German prisoner, then me guarding that prisoner, then another prisoner, and one of the fellows guarding him, and then the rest of the guys. We had hardly left the tree line when I broke through an ice bridge that was over a creek. I accidentally threw my rifle right up to where the prisoner was, and fell into the creek to about a 2 to 3 foot depth. I scrambled out as fast as I could and picked up my rifle which the German had not touched. He still held his hands behind his head. Others fell into the creek. It was a mess.

We finally were all together again and went on. It was still snowing, and my pants froze. But we went on, and on, and on. We stopped finally and called in with our radio. We asked for a flare to get our bearings. Boehme felt we should have come to our lines by now. They shot the flare, but we did not see it. We started again.

"Bang" behind me. The German fell to the ground, shot accidentally by our man who had his finger on the trigger of his pistol. His finger had become so cold he could not feel it and so had wiggled it and accidentally pulled the trigger. The other prisoner seemed to think we had done this on purpose. He held his hands extra high. Boehme was afraid that the shot had been heard, and felt men would come out after us, so said we had to *get moving*! But he was exhausted, since he had been first and plowed the way through the snow for the rest of us. And the snow had been knee high in places. He gave me the compass and told me the direction to go. He said he would bring up the rear. He feared discovery from that area. He was a good man and always did what was needed. Both being Lutherans, we had also become acquaintances.

As instructed, I led on, and on, and on—following the direction the compass pointed. For some reason I felt like I should be going to the right of where the compass pointed. But I knew that this happened when you were using a compass and that I must trust the compass, especially since it was snowing and I had no other way of knowing where to go. We finally stopped again. We asked for a flare. We saw nothing. But while standing and waiting for the flare I noticed a very large cable on the ground. I pointed this out to Boehme and said it looked to me as if we had walked through the first line of defense, and the second line of defense, and were standing in the Battalion headquarters area. He agreed and asked that a flare be shot up over the Battalion Headquarters. The flare went off, and there we were standing in the light of the flare, right outside of Colonel Douglas's headquarters. (See Map 2)

He came boiling out of his domed fortress, and stood there looking at us under the fading light of the flare. He was very upset. He realized that if we could get through two lines of defense so could the enemy. Yet he was also mighty glad to see us, especially with the prisoner. He immediately had us come into his headquarters, which had a nice coal stove burning away in the center of it. By domed fortress I mean that the Colonel's headquarters was so constructed with wooden supports, beams and wood roofing, all covered with several feet of dirt, that it probably could have withstood a fairly large shell hitting it and not getting through to do harm. It must have been about 15 or 20 feet in diameter. Those of us who were wet from falling in the stream dried out, and then very reluctantly went back to our holes. It was so nice and warm in the Colonel's "fortress." But someone had to be on the front line, and so back to our holes we went. It had been one very eventful evening. But the next day would also be most interesting.

It seems that the German had been interrogated. As he spoke he said how surprised he had been to find out that they had been fighting black troops. "I have no black troops," insisted Colonel Douglas. "But black men just captured me," the German said. So the Colonel went up to the front lines in order to see just what it was that the German prisoner was talking about. Well, we had been burning gasoline in our holes, and our faces, necks, and hair were black with soot, even the backs of our hands were black. He then understood the problem and told every one of us, "You men are to go back as soon as possible and get showers and come back here clean. I will not have this." Well, we sure weren't opposed to the idea of getting clean.

And so it was that I soon had my turn at going back and getting a shower. We ended up in a place in Verviers, I believe, about 4:00 or 5:00 p.m., just a little before sundown. We were tired and asked if we could just lie down on the floor for a nap. "Go ahead," we were told. The next minute I was awakened. It was light, so I thought only a few minutes had gone by. "Are you kidding," said the clerk. "It is 7:30 a.m. You guys have slept like the dead for over 12 hours." Well, something told me that what he said was true. Anyway, we got our showers. I soaped up and scrubbed four or five times before my freckles and red hair reappeared. After a time we all got back to the outfit. Now, remember, our outfit was all replacements since we had gone on line in front of Elsenborn. So I walked up to the men and said, "Hello," and not one man recognized me at first. One, "You're so young." Another, "Hey, you have red hair and freckles." Still another, "We wouldn't even know you if it were not for your voice and being so tall."

In a letter dated January 19, 1945, I write: Dear Mom and Dad, **"I'm on a 24 hour pass for a shower and a good night's sleep. The shower was wonderful. We went to (name of town censored out) for the shower. It was a civilian operated place."**

About this time we were told that a big patrol was going to go across our front and attack into the woods. We saw them go in and then a lot of firing commenced. A little later we were told to watch for them, that they were coming back. Pretty soon we saw them, and the artillery laid smoke between them and the Germans. Then suddenly the Germans started to shell us. Some medics who had just gotten to our outpost, on their way to help the injured in the patrol came running back. Four of them jumped into our hole, breaking the wrist of a fellow named Shanger. I was very angry at this. The Lt. told me to go out and guide the patrol in. I got to the outpost just in time to see the patrol start to take a short cut. They did not realize we had a mine field in that area. We yelled at them to not cross that area. Then "boom," and two men went down. We got the rest on the right path and then took a sled out to the downed men. One fellow got up and said he was only slightly hit in one arm. The other fellow had a foot blown off and an arm broken. He only worried about his arm. He didn't realize he was hit anywhere else. We put him on the sled, pulled him back to the lines, and then to the medics. It was so cold that he hadn't bled but a few drops.

Writing about that month or so in our foxholes, waiting for spring, when we could finish the job of conquering the enemy, I recall that the hardest thing were the nights. Later, in 1945, I wrote about this:

**"Then came the darkness. First I went around with the password, then a little later I went around with information about any patrols of ours, and when and where they would be seen. We did this so the fellows wouldn't get scared and fire at them as they went past. Then came the all night vigil. Nights were twice as long as the day, and the Lord knows that the days were long enough."**

Why did I say the nights were twice as long as the days? It is because we were short of men and there were only two of us in each hole. This meant standing guard for two hours, then changing places and sleeping two hours, and then getting up and standing guard two hours while the other fellow slept, etc. The result was that each night seemed to turn one day into three or four days.

Toward the end of January it starting snowing and did not let up. I wrote:

**"Then it started snowing, snowing, snowing, until it was hip deep in every spot, other than our trails. All night we took turns keeping the snow out of the hole. We would sweat while working and then just about freeze when we stopped. And it was no use trying to put on our overcoats. They had all frozen solid and were useless. We had found it best to forget them and instead put on another pair of pants and shirt."**

At this time we were wearing one set of long johns, one set of wool pants and shirt, a wool sweater, and one set of waterproof pants and shirt. The last item we put on was a waterproof field jacket. For foot wear I always wore the usual—two pairs of socks with my feet inside my boots from which I had cut out the toe section, and then wore the boots inside the waterproof overshoes. With all of these in place, I was usually fairly warm and comfortable.

The Story of the 394th Infantry says of this time, "From Dec. 29 to Jan. 31 action was limited to patrolling." The severe weather is also mentioned in a Citation awarded the 99th Infantry Division under the signature of CHARLES, Prince of Belgium, where it says, "The Division took a defensive position on the Elsenborn crest and checked all the enemy attacks under extremely difficult climatic conditions until the 30th January 1945 when the Division was again able to take the offensive." (Lauer, p.151)

## ON THE ATTACK TO THE RHINE
## FEBRUARY 1 - MARCH 17, 1945

In early February we were told to roll up everything. We were moving out. Thank God! So we rolled up the little we had—two blankets (we left the rest), socks, handkerchiefs, soap, razor, poncho, pen and pencil, but not much else—and a pack to carry it in. The rest was all in a rear area.

But it did include our frozen overcoats. We put a string through the top buttonhole and then tied the other end of the string to our belts and actually dragged the coats behind us. They had all gotten wet and froze into whatever shape they had last been in, and sometimes in peculiar shapes at that. Frozen as they were, they were just one big bother. But we were all responsible for all our equipment; so there we were, dutifully dragging these big heavy frozen overcoats behind us. When some big shot finally saw this "parade of the coats," he about had a fit. He quickly had all the coats collected, and that was the end of that. We finally got back to Elsenborn. But the hike had been murderous, since the ground was so slippery. Then they took us by truck to some camp in the woods where we stayed overnight. Next day they moved us to a place where we were to rest. All day we worked like dogs building log cabins so we could sleep in them that night, which we did. The next day they took us to a place where we could take showers. It was the second one I had had in two months. We finally got back to our newly-built cabins, only to be told to roll it up. We were being sent to new positions, but in reserve. After just building the cabins, now abandon them? "Don't worry. We are to take over some other outfit's holes."

It snowed something awful during that week. Then suddenly it got warm. We had been afraid of this happening because we knew it would melt the snow. Then the water would work through the earth that was on top of the sleeping part of our holes and we would get wet. And this is just what happened. It was an absolutely miserable situation.

Orders came to get ready to jump off in an attack. Next morning we moved out on the attack. It seems that the Jerries were beating such a fast retreat that we could not keep up with them. We found that they were trying to escape encirclement. That night we pushed aside the snow and lay down and tried to sleep. Very few slept because it was so cold it made you cry to stay in one place or position too long. In the morning some of the fellows had to be picked up and worked on before they could move. Finally the orders came to build fires, and that is what we did. Later we heard that the Germans had made good their escape.

One interesting thing happened during this attempt to catch up to the retreating Germans and encircle them. As we went along, we finally did pass one area where a little fighting had taken place, and a few dead German soldiers lay by the side of the road. After we had passed this area one of the men in our platoon came up to me and said, "Sarge, I've got a problem. I was cleaning my rifle and the string broke and the cleaning plug is in the barrel." (We had cleaning items in a well in the wooden shoulder piece of our rifle. It consisted of a string about 3-feet long with a split piece of metal on one end into which a cleaning patch could be placed. A small weight on the other end of the string could be put into the breach of the rifle so it would fall through the barrel and out the front end. You then pulled the cleaning patch through the barrel and thus cleaned it. But it was tricky. If you did not do everything just right, the patch would jam the barrel, and this is what had happened to him. So instead of carefully restarting his cleaning process, he had pulled hard on the string, and it had broken.) So here, when it looks as if we might go into battle at any moment, he brings this to my attention. Of course he was worried, since if he pulled the trigger with the barrel plugged the rifle might explode and he could be hurt, or blinded, or who knows what. I gave him my rifle and told him I would be right back. What I did was walk back along the line of moving troops until I found a machine gunner. They had steel rods with which they cleaned the machine guns. One of the gunners lent me his steel-cleaning rod, and I was able to shove out the stuck patch. Then I took the gun back to the man and got my rifle back. (Just an added note. This particular soldier always seemed to be in trouble. I sometimes wonder whatever happened to him.)

The next day we got on 2 1/2-ton trucks and moved up to our old positions at Losheimergraben. It snowed on the way up, but it didn't bother us much. We had come to relieve the 82nd Airborne Division. They told us that all was quiet, so we pitched tents. Besides, holes were useless, since it was so warm the snow was melting and getting into a hole was like jumping into a swimming pool. We were allowed to build fires, so we made ourselves comfortable. The official history of the 394th says of this time, "By the first of February the little Belgian and German towns in which the 394th fought so bitterly during the Nazis' Ardennes offensive had been retaken by American troops. Honsfeld, Bullingen, Murringen, Krinkelt, Hunningen, Wirtzfeld and Losheimergrabben were all free again. . . . On Feb. 4, the 394th relieved the 82nd Airborne Div. in the Neuhof and Losheim areas. . . . An unexpectedly early thaw that turned roads into canals of mud made the Battle of Supply and of cleaning minefields major ones."

On February 8, I wrote my parents:

"I received a letter from our old platoon Sergeant. He is in England with trench foot, so is Sergeant Davies my old squad leader."

On February 9:

". . . Well, to think that I would have been through 2 years of college now instead of 2 years of seeing the U.S. and Europe as a soldier. Sure is a big difference. I just wonder which would or will be the best. I know that I have learned an awful lot that I never would have otherwise."

On February 12:

"I don't need a watch any more. I took one from a German that didn't need it any more. I also have a P-38 pistol. . . . Everything seems to be going okay with me."

On February 24:

**"They made me a Staff Sergeant today. I just hope that I can fill the bill. If the platoon leader gets put out of commission I have to take over, otherwise I take care of different jobs in the platoon."** *(A platoon is about 40 men. At this time Sergeant Nichols was Platoon Sergeant. We had no officer, so the two of us took care of the platoon.)*

I also answered a question my mother had asked:

**"Well, Mom, we took a lot of that mortar fire, etc., for a long time and I have thanked God many times that I made it through without a scratch. We were hit by 5 Nazi Divisions in that German push."**

Some time during this period of so much moving about, we were put into a rather nice home. We all made ourselves comfortable, and some of us also did what every soldier did regular with his M-l. He cleaned and oiled it and ended up with a bullet in the chamber and the safety lock on. The safety lock on the M-l is just ahead of the trigger guard, so you must be sure you finger is on the trigger lock and not the trigger when you put on the safety. Well, I was not careful, and so when I pulled hard to put the safety on, BANG. Of course, the guys all jumped up and wanted to know what the hell I thought I was doing. I had to admit the error of my ways, but I can also say that I was mighty thankful I had been putting on the safety "according to the book" -namely, by making sure the rifle was pointing up. I just hoped no one was upstairs. No one was.

I had broken my glasses in January and now decided

that I had better go back and get some new ones. Nothing was happening, so I figured I sure wouldn't be missed. I went back by ambulance to a collecting company and from there to an evacuation hospital. There a doctor got me a prescription. From there I caught a ride to Dalheim, Belgium, where they made the glasses in about 15 minutes. Then I went to the 99th Division rear area at Verviers and stayed overnight. The next day I started back on the mail truck and got back to the company. I tell all of this because it was interesting to me that during the war, and even for a good time afterwards, all of the G.I.'s would help each other with transportation or anything else you needed. Also, I must say that as long as the war was on the front line troops got a lot of respect and all the help they wanted. I sometimes felt the help was so readily given because the troops in the rear were so happy we were on the front lines, and not they, that they wanted to make sure we were happy and well supplied so that it would be less likely they would have to go to the front. Well, I really did not blame them for thinking that way.

The next day we moved back for a rest. We got a nice room in a school building, and for 3 days all we did was just sleep and eat real food, not K rations. But we could not take regular rations after eating K rations for so long, so we all got the runs (dysentery).

Lt. Conrath, our C.O. since December 20, told a group of us that we were to go with him to look for quarters near St. Pierre. The company was to go there for more rest. St. Pierre is near Aubel, Belgium. We found a place and in due time our company moved in. We did little for several weeks other than clean up equipment, eat, and generally take it easy. We were near a castle, and that was an interesting place to look at. Our regimental history says of this time, "On Feb. 8 the 394th pulled back to an assembly area 1,000 yards west of Losheimergraben and stayed there till the 12th when it left for a 19-day 'rest' near the Belgium towns of Waimes and Aubel."

On February 27, they gave us maps. An all-out offensive had already started, and we were to be part of it. The maps were of an area around a town named Elsdorf. The map showed a lot of fortification and trenches. Things looked as if they were going to be rough.

The next day they took us by truck to a field near Elsdorf. Here we were with the artillery, so we were way back of the front lines. We could see far ahead where they were fighting, and it looked like rough going. The official records say, "On Mar. 2 the 394th moved out of the Aubel area headed east. Big events lay ahead. . . . The 394th had seen its last defensive action. 'Attack!' was the word that filled every official order and every doughboy's mind. . . . The 99th was the first American division to reach the Rhine."

At about 2100 (9 p.m.) on March 2 or 3, they told us to make up our packs with a blanket and a poncho. (Each poncho was an 8x8, or so, foot piece of plastic-like material with a hole in the center big enough for your head to go through. It was warm to wear and it kept out the rain.) Then they issued each of us 3 K rations (day's supply).

We then walked about 2 miles to the Erft Canal which we crossed by bridge. The job of the 394th was to secure a portion of the Cologne Plain about 5 miles wide and 12 miles long ending at the Rhine. We first came to rail yards, and since it was late in the day, rolled up in our blankets and ponchos and remained there until the next morning. It was very cold, and we found ourselves waking up about every hour to get warm enough to sleep again. We shoved off at about 0700. Our objective was the third town down the road from us. On our right we could see our tanks moving up. We had tanks with us, and there were more to our left. Planes were overhead, and artillery was booming away behind us, shelling the enemy in front of us. We felt like we were all-powerful, but I knew good and well that one mortar shell could stop us at least for a time.

We finally came to the town we were to take. It offered no resistance, but the officers were sure that the Germans would counter-attack. So they had us go from house to house and tell the civilians to get out so they would not have artillery fall on them. I wrote home about this on April 19, 1945, and said:

**"I was just thinking about the way some of the German civilians acted when we swept through their towns. The usual procedure is to send them to the rear so that if the Germans started shelling us they won't get hurt. . . . so, there was an old man by a door when I came and told him to head for the rear.** *(They understand sign language when you use a rifle to make the sign.)* **Well, he started wringing his hands and weeping. He then showed me inside the door, where stood two females with a flock of kids not old enough to walk, and all crying hysterically. I shoved the man inside and said, 'O.K., O.K.' because I doubted very much if the Germans would shell us**

because they were in too much of a hurry, running. Well, all of the people started saying *'danka, danka'* (thanks, thanks), as I left."

My thought proved to be correct since the Germans did not counter-attack but kept retreating toward the Rhine. The next town was at a distance, so the 1st Platoon got on the tanks and rode ahead. (I was in the 3rd Platoon.) The town was supposed to be "no problem," but when we got near, German tanks appeared and began shooting at our tanks. All of a sudden one of ours got hit, and then another. Rifle and mortar fire also came in. One tank with 7 men on it got a direct hit with a mortar. It killed two or three and injured the rest. We were in reserve for the company so were a little behind all this action, but suddenly we began to take a lot of artillery and mortar fire. We tried to move up, but were stopped cold. The word came that our Company Commander, Lt. Conrath, had been killed. He was one of the best officers we had. Now we realized why everything had suddenly come to a halt.

Then, suddenly, a tank near us was hit with mortar fire. The officer in charge of the tank was standing in the turret when the mortar shell hit. It sliced off his body from the waist at an angle through the top part of his body. So his body was "standing" there in the tank minus his head, etc. What was left was one bloody mess. It was awful. The uninjured members of the tank crew abandoned the tank. We urged them to go back and do what they had to since we needed their help. But they would not go back. We didn't argue with them. We saw how upset they were.

We finally went on into town, checked it out for soldiers, and then went on to the next town. Here a lot of German soldiers just surrendered by walking out of the homes with their hands up. It made things a lot easier that way. Finally at dusk we came up to another town. We were told to halt. We all lay down in the field where we had stopped. It slowly got dark. It was quiet for some reason. We had been going night and day for at least two days. We all went to sleep. Suddenly I realized I had gone to sleep. I looked around and I realized everyone was asleep. "Sleeping in the midst of battle? This is not good," I thought to myself. Lt. Rhodes had taken over as Company Commander, and he saw the situation. We woke up all the guys and moved into town. Groups were given houses and told to get into the cellars and get some rest since we would be taking off early in the morning. When we moved in we found that the Germans must have been living in their cellars, since beds were there, all made up. We made the most of it and got a good night's rest.

The next day we regrouped and headed toward the Rhine. We went along a railroad that went east toward the Rhine and met no opposition. We came to a large barn and farmhouse and formed two columns, each headed east. We were to go forward some distance, and then one platoon was to go right and the other left. When all the men were in line parallel to the Rhine, we were to face toward the Rhine and advance in a flank attack. So here we were, one platoon all lined up beginning at the front of the barn, and heading east, and the other group of us all lined up beginning at the back part of the barn and heading east, all ready to go forward. It was at this time when the two columns were about 50 feet apart that we all heard a loud THUD toward the front of the columns. It was an immense artillery shell which proceeded to travel down between the two columns, go up the sloping earth which was along the side of the barn, travel a ways up the wall of the barn, fall back and go down the slope to finally stop in about the middle of the two columns. And what had we done all this time? We had all just stood there watching, mesmerized by the sight of that immense shell that could wipe us all out, rather than doing what we should have done, hit the dirt. Thank God it was a dud, or many of us most likely would have been killed.

We now went forward and formed up alongside the field, all facing east in the direction of the Rhine. We could see our tanks and troops to our right and left. Airplanes were overhead. Artillery again was in the rear giving us good support. We felt absolutely invincible as we went forward. But when we were about halfway across the field, machine guns opened up on us. We hit the dirt. The man next to me got up to run forward a little, but a bullet had cut his belt. So as he stood, it did not come with him, and he circled and came back for it, and was hit. I yelled for the medic. The medic did not come. I didn't blame him, since I was trying to burrow into the ground or find some high spot to hide behind. The machine gun fire was murderous, and the worst was that no one could see where it was coming from. More than one man got hit.

But someone did see. One of our planes suddenly dived on the barn that stood well in front of us on the edge of the town. He dropped a bomb on the barn, and out lumbered a great big German tank. Here it had been inside the barn and shooting at us through the open doors. It was so black inside the barn that neither we nor any of our anti-tank guys had seen him. And so off he went like some giant who was not to be pushed around. The plane took another crack at him, and a German gunner on the tank shot back. The tracers could plainly be seen. The German gunner seemed to be spraying the plane with bullets while the pilot of the plane shot back and kept right on diving toward the tank, shooting away for all he was worth even though it looked like the plane was surely being hit. But he must not have been hit, or hit seriously, since he flew off, while the German tank majestically progressed down the road into the town.

We had lost several men, killed and wounded, but since the wounded were being taken care of we went on into the town. I saw a shoe in the street, and when I got close, I saw there was a foot still in it. I could not help wonder just what had happened, since nothing else was anywhere around. We met no other resistance, and since the town was close to the Rhine, we stayed to "mop up." That means going to every home making sure no soldiers were there to give us trouble. The civilians knew they had best be on their good behavior. The one thing I remember about that operation was going into one home and noticing that the man of the house was very nervous. So we looked around and finally asked him if there were any guns we had not spotted. He was sweating heavily by now and took us into the basement and dug in the dirt just behind the basement stairs. There was a pistol. He handed it over, and we thanked him.

The history of the 394th says, "Every day from Mar. 3 on was Flag Day for Germans - 'White Flag Day'. . . . On the 4th they continued their pace, and on the 5th when they pulled up to the Rhine between Dusseldorf and Cologne, the 394th had slashed 12 miles and taken

19 towns." On March 7, we were handed the following commendation from our Regimental Commander:

*Headquarters, 99th Infantry Division
APO 449, U S ARMY*

MEMORANDUM:

TO: All officers and men of my Regiment.

*You, the fighting men of the 394th Infantry, have again demonstrated your superiority over the enemy.*

*Between 0750, 3 March 45 and 0900, 5 March 45, you advanced approximately 22,000 yards into enemy territory, capturing 19 towns and villages. Your aggressive advance was halted only by receipt of another mission.*

*396 prisoners were taken and 3 tanks and 1 self-propelled gun were knocked out or captured; also many mortars and small arms in good condition were captured by you which is indicative of the zeal with which you performed your task. Superior performance of duty by each of you led to success for the Regiment.*

*I take this opportunity as your Regimental Commander to express my pride in you and my gratitude for your gallant action.*

*J. R. Jeter
Colonel, Infantry
Commanding.*

## REMAGEN BRIDGEHEAD
## MARCH 9 - MARCH 17, 1945

A rumor was making the rounds that the 9th Armored Division had captured the railroad bridge that crossed the Rhine River at Remagen. We sure hoped this was true, for we had already begun sweating it out. We did not want to go across the Rhine on a boat while being shot at. On March 9 we heard the dramatic news that on March 7 the 9th Division had indeed captured the bridge, and that since we were so close we were to go there immediately.

The cooks brought up all of our equipment, we were put aboard trucks, and off we went in the middle of the night toward Remagen. And here SOP (Standard Operating Procedure) was being followed. Before combat we put all our stuff together in our field pack and took it to the cooks. (They had the trucks.) All we took into combat was our rifle, ammunition, and web belt from which was hung a bayonet, water canteen, first aid kit, and entrenching tool. (Sometimes we also carried a light pack with blanket, poncho, and extra rations.) When not in combat we were given back all of our stuff and were expected to take care of it, which included sending dirty socks, etc., off to the laundry when told to do so.

So here we were traveling along in a truck convoy to the Remagen area. As we went along PFC Sherwood Henry began talking about a dream he kept having. His dream was that we would soon be coming to a hilly part of Germany and make an attack down a valley into a city and all get shot up and all killed. This led into a discussion of dreams. Some of us maintained that dreams just showed what a person was thinking about, and since all of us were thinking about getting killed, a dream like Henry's was just a natural thing. But he insisted God revealed the future to him through dreams. We could not convince him otherwise but dropped the subject, since his dream was not a very pleasant or encouraging one.

At last we got to an area near Remagen, and were dropped off. (See Map 3) Even in the middle of the night we could tell that men and equipment from all over had been brought into the area. We just laid a blanket on the ground, put our poncho over us, and went to sleep. And even though it rained we got a fairly good night's rest.

The next day we moved into a barn with an artillery unit. They gave us everything they could spare in the way of hot chow and coffee. I don't know why our cooks were not around. We spent the day cleaning weapons, getting ammunition, and doing everything else needed for crossing the river. About 9 p.m., just as we were planning to go to sleep, they told us to pack up because we were to cross the river. We packed everything. Nothing was to go on vehicles because they wanted to get as much equipment across the Rhine as possible. They were going to use us as pack mules, in a sense, but we realized that it was for our own good. Some of the guys griped about it, but that was the way it always was. Griping seemed to make some of the guys feel better.

We all put on our full packs, and off we went. Of course

it rained. And we walked, and walked, and walked. Sgt. Nichols led the column, and I brought up the rear and tried to keep everyone together. Even at that a few fellows dropped out. We really were not used to carrying all of our equipment. We finally took a slow curving road that led down to the river and the city of Remagen. (See Map 3) The snake-like column of troops and half-tracks mounted with 50-caliber machine guns, and vehicles pulling artillery pieces, could be seen in the artillery flashes. It was awesome to say the least. We were on the attack now and we felt good that we were part of something that was strong and good and invincible.

The Germans were shelling Remagen regularly. Of course, they knew the town and what we had to do to cross the bridge. So what they were doing was shelling it at the choke point where the vehicles and men had to join in order to get onto the bridge. We were marched down a side street and told we would have to wait our turn. It was raining and cold, so it was just plain miserable. I finally sat on my helmet, keeping just the helmet liner on my head, and put the poncho over my liner so I was in a "tent" and tried to sleep sitting up. At least I was warm. And all this time shells would come screaming by and hit whatever was crossing the road at that moment. Trucks were hit. And what was done? A bulldozer would just push the disabled truck aside and the next truck or troops would go by. The driver? I really don't remember, but I suppose they were pulled out. But finally someone got wise to the Germans. They noted that the Germans were shooting 4 rounds, and then 8 seconds would go by before the next 4 rounds. So they had a man counting time, and the moment the 4th round hit, men ran across that spot, or the vehicles went by, and at the count of 7 all stopped. A gap was left where the shells had been hitting. The 4 rounds would hit, but now hit nothing. When the last shell landed, we again had 8 seconds for troops or trucks to make the bridge. And it worked, thanks to the Germans being so methodical.

*The Ludendorf Railroad Bridge at Remagen, Germany. (Note the German prisoners at left, facing toward us. Our outfit ran over this bridge at night, March 12, 1945.)*

Finally our turn came. We rushed by the spot on the double, and shortly found ourselves going down an incline to the bottom of one of the two big towers which supported the bridge. Then we went up the spiral staircase to the roadbed. Then off we went, running across the bridge in the dark, trying to make sure we did not step in any of the holes that had been made by the bombs which had been used to bring down the bridge. I finally came to the east side of the bridge which ran into a tunnel, since the east side of the Rhine in that area is hilly. The west side of the Rhine in that area is fairly flat land. As I entered the tunnel I looked up the cliff and saw how rugged the hillside was and wondered how the fellows had ever taken this place. It looked impossible to me.

It was here in the railroad tunnel that our company formed up. Right away we noticed that we were not alone. There were also a number of German civilians taking refuge in the tunnel. Well, we didn't blame them. In "The Story of the 394th Infantry" it says, "The story of the crossing of the Rhine by the 394th, one of the first units over, is one of individual heroism of men risking their lives to keep traffic flowing over the bridge, to treat and evacuate casualties, and to rally the shell-dazed soldiers."

The walking to get to Remagen, the wait for our turn to get across the bridge, the running across the bridge, and the forming up again in the tunnel took almost all night. So it was that early the next morning we moved out along a road built into the steep side of the hill on the east side of the Rhine. As we walked along we found ourselves walking along a two-lane road with half-tracks and other vehicles on each side of the road. The half-tracks were mounted with 50-caliber machine guns, or 20-mm ack-ack guns. These vehicles were bumper-to-bumper, leaving only one lane between them just wide enough for a truck or troops to travel between them. I was amazed to see that so much equipment had made it across, and somewhat apprehensive about what would happen if the Germans mounted a counter-offensive. We were all so close together. But we soon saw why all the half-tracks with the guns were there. A German plane came over, trying to bomb the bridge into the river to keep us from using it. All the gunners opened up. What a noise. But they did not hit the bomber. The bomber made its bombing run, but it did not manage to hit the bridge as far as we could tell. But we did experience what happens when so many bullets are shot into the air. It began to rain spent bullets. Of course this could be dangerous if you were looking up. So we tried to stand straight and tall to make as little a target as possible. A few bullets hit fellows on their helmets, but no one came to any harm.

And then we saw something none of us could at first believe. We thought surely our seeing was being deceived in some way, for a German plane was flying over at a tremendous speed, but it had no propeller. We were seeing our first jet plane. We all stood and watched the show, since now several of our air-planes were in the area trying to keep the German planes from bombing the bridge. As we watched several fellows said, "Ah, yes, we Americans have the best and the finest and the latest weapons available." (The officers would regularly tell us this.) But now this jet. And the jet was after our planes, trying to shoot them down so their bombers could bomb the bridge. We watched as a jet attacked a P-38. As you perhaps know, a P-38 had one lower wing, but two fuselages separated by some space. Well, the jet was going so fast compared to the speed of the P-38, that the pilot did not pull up quickly enough. So, as he shot at the P-38, he went through the space between the two sections of the P-38. This, of course, cut off the whole back section of the P-38, the jet lost its wings, and both planes went down. Much to our surprise we soon saw two parachutes.

Our company continued to walk along the road. We stopped by the roadside to eat some K rations. We then went about two miles into a small town. Each platoon was given permission to find a home and take a break. Nick (Sgt. Nichols, our Platoon Sergeant) found us a place, and we all made ourselves at home. We were all dead tired. Nevertheless we did not sleep. We just started to cook everything we could find, since there was food in the house. Nick and I found a room by ourselves because we always had work to do, and we did not want to have someone bothering us. We had to look over the maps we were given, make reports about anyone missing, give permission for guys to go on sick call and tell them where to go, get ammunition if needed, and make sure everyone was "happy." At this time we were giving out extra ammunition that was brought to us in bandoleer form. The M-1 was fed by a clip containing 8 rounds. The bandoleers were wide cloth belts with little pockets in them that held about 10 of these clips. You could then put them around your neck like a person might carry binoculars. While attending to such matters, I got some eggs and stew cooking, and Nick and I had a nice meal. We could always seem to eat.

That afternoon we fell out and went through the town looking for weapons and anything else that the Germans might have that could be used against us. The boys naturally took everything of any value, such as watches, jewelry, and many pistols. Money was uncertain so usually left alone. We all slept good that night. In the morning things were uncertain, so we got a little more rest and a lot of speculation as to the future.

We moved out that afternoon. The 2nd and 3rd Battalions were now going to attack the Germans who were trying to push us back across the Rhine. Our battalion was put in reserve. The idea was that if either battalion got into trouble, we would then be able to quickly come up and help them. As we marched along to get into position, we went by a German winery. As we went by, each fellow was given a bottle of wine and told to drink up. Well, I remember that I did not really think this was a very good idea since a person needs to think straight when in battle. But perhaps the officers realized what was in store for us and wanted to give us a little false courage. So, there we were, following behind another battalion who was making progress in their attack, and drinking wine as we walked along.

To appreciate the situation, and what follows, one needs to have a picture of the terrain and our organizational set-up. As before said, the west side of the Rhine near Remagen is fairly flat. But the east side is very hilly, and the hills are covered with fir trees and all kinds of other trees and bushes. Among these hills, in the valleys, are small towns. One fairly good-sized town on the east side of the Rhine, up the river from Remagen, (south, since the Rhine runs north) was Honningen. (See Map 3) Our 394th Regiment now had the job of fighting for and taking over the hills around Honningen, and then taking Honningen itself. To do this our four battalions which made up the 394th Infantry Regiment were going into action. Remember that a company is about 180 men when at full strength. We were down to about two-thirds of that. First Battalion would be Companies A, B, C, D. Second Battalion would be Companies E, F, G, H. Third Battalion would be Companies I, K, L, M, (no J). We were Company "A." Companies are made up of 4 platoons, and each platoon is supposed to have 40 men, including an officer. Our platoon only had non-commissioned officers since the Battle of the Bulge.

So picture to yourself our little 3rd Platoon of Company A (about 30 men), walking out of the little town, wine bottles in hand, ready to do whatever we were told. Being part of the reserve, we were feeling fairly good about everything. Then suddenly we are told that our company was now part of the attack force, since the hill country into which we were walking was full of Germans, and the other two battalions had their hands full.

Well, what could we do but just keep on walking? We soon ran out of road and began going up what I would call a "hogback," that is, the top part of a slowly rising hill. The hogback had parts that were narrow but also parts that were fairly wide. In these wide areas there were not only large fir trees but also grassy areas. We came to what we soon learned was the top of the hill. It had narrow places, dropping off on both sides, but also wider places. It was being defended by some German troops. Our men began firing and calling for artillery to help them. The Germans did likewise, so we found ourselves under a tremendous artillery barrage. Our fellows decided that by having our artillery stop and us attack, we would get out from under their barrage and also take the hilltop. This was done and we drove the Germans off the hilltop. At this time our platoon was in reserve for the company, so we heard all of the commotion, but at first did not know just what was happening. Suddenly all guns stopped firing. Hardly had they stopped when wounded were gathered and carried back. One of them was Sgt. Boehme. An artillery shell had landed next to him and cut open the upper part of his leg so that it looked just like a piece of raw meat. However, no major artery had been hit, so he was not in too great a danger. I saw all of this as he was being carried along on a stretcher by four guys, at shoulder height. He was hanging on to the edges of the stretcher as if he was afraid he might fall off, but otherwise he was his usual uncomplaining self. He was a very good man. I hated to see him hit and have to be evacuated.

It was now getting late. The officers began posting everyone around the edge of the hilltop. We knew we had to dig in and be ready for a counter-attack, since we were holding some of the high ground overlooking the city of Honningen. Our platoon was assigned an area that fronted a heavily wooded slope that ended in a small valley dominated by a large farm house. While Sgt. Nichols was seeing to rations and all, I was told to place the men. So I went along the edge of the hilltop telling the men where to dig. The Germans had some holes already dug, and we tried to make use of them. I finally came to a place where three of our men had found a very nice hole already dug. But the problem was that it was about 20 feet in front of our other holes, and slightly down the hillside. I told the guys they would just have to come back up to the top and dig in line with the others. If they stayed where they were and we got into a fight, we might shoot them in the back. "Oh, no, we will be O.K. Look how deep this hole is. We will put dirt in back of us." I insisted that they come back in line with the rest of us, and so they finally did, very angry with me. Especially they were angry because the ground was very hard. Nick and I found a nice big hole that was unusually deep and large, but it was back of the rest of the men and perfect for us so that we could be in position to help anyone who was in trouble in case of a counter-attack.

Night came, and remember, this is probably about March 15. We ate K rations for supper. Then we checked that everyone was in place and had water and ammunition and everything else they needed. Then we tried to get some sleep. This means one man wide awake in each hole, the other two trying to sleep.

About midnight a fellow came back to where we were and said they could hear men coming up through the trees. It sounded as if this were true. So the fellow went back to his place, and we called for artillery to begin just in front of our lines and march forward. The artillery came but landed on us. It happened that another fellow had just then come to tell us it sounded like Germans were coming up his side of the slope, so when the shells landed he was blown in right on top of us, but not hurt. Of course we grabbed the phone and told the artillery guys what they were doing. Shortly they elevated their guns and put the rounds in the right place. We understood their problem since they were shooting to hit the down side of a slope and the distance between us and where we wanted the shells was actually a very short distance on the flat, but of course much longer on the slope. We were very thankful that none of our fellows got hit.

The rest of the night went by with all of us still very fearful of a counter-attack. But none came. Finally dawn came. About an hour or so after dawn the three men I had made dig a new hole, rather than use the one down the side of the hill came to me. They hardly had gotten to where I was standing than they all fell down on their knees in front of me and bowed at the waist as if I were some kind of a god. It was very upsetting to be so treated, and I asked them just what had gotten into them. They signaled that I should come with them, which I did. We came to their hole, and they pointed to where they had wanted to stay. It had received a direct hit, and was now a much bigger and deeper hole than before. If they had been there, they would have all been blown to bits. I told them they should thank God, not me, for I was just doing my duty. Their answer to that was, "Sarge, from now on, whatever you tell us to do, we'll do."

I have thought of that particular incident many times since. Of course, the artillery shell could have landed in the new hole I had made them dig. I have come to a conclusion you might not agree with. My conclusion is that God wonderfully blesses what is right. What I told the men to do was the right thing.

Nothing much happened that morning other than discovering that there were Germans in the farm house in the meadow below us. Not only that, another part of our battalion was on the hill across from us. This meant there was a gap in our line and that the Germans could use the farm house as a staging area at night to pour troops up the valley between us and into the forest and around in back of us. And if either group of us were attacked from both front and back, even though we held high ground, we could be in big trouble. Or we could be isolated and just starved out.

What should we do? After lunch I was told, "Mac, get a squad together. You have been given the job of taking that farm house." My heart fell. What this meant was attacking over about a football field of open ground before actually getting to the house. I could just see us being mowed down like hay before a mowing machine. But since I had the job, I went down the hill and got as close to the farm house as I dared. Getting close I could see the job was not going to be easy, regardless of how we did it. We would just have to attack across the field. There was no other way.

As I started back through the trees a fellow came to me and said, "Forget it. Some fellows have volunteered to take the farm house." Better news I had never heard. Then I saw some of the best soldiering I ever saw. Way to the right of me, at the end of the meadow where I had figured we would have to begin our attack, some men were crawling up, spreading out behind the trees. They began their attack, and they did it right. They had spread out so they were about 10 feet from one another. At command every other man got up and charged straight forward, making no attempt to shoot. The other men shot between them at windows or doors from which the enemy might shoot. Then the men who had run forward, about 50 feet from where they had started, hit the ground, and started shooting as the other men got up and ran forward, running between the men firing. They then hit the dirt about 50 feet in front of the men who were firing their weapons, etc. This is a very dangerous form of attack, and very difficult, since the usual way of attacking is to run forward in a zigzag path so the enemy cannot get an easy shot at you. They continued this form of attack with great skill and daring. It was obvious that they were a very disciplined group and knew their business.

They were about 100 feet from the farm house when white shirts began to be waved out the windows and doors along with the cry, "Comrade." This was what the Germans said when they surrendered. Soon they had all the Germans out. Then some of the men started walking toward us shouting, "Hey, you'all have some ammunition, we'all have bout run out." I could hardly believe my eyes. The men were all blacks. They were a group of black fellows who had volunteered to fight as infantry soldiers to prove that a colored American was just as good a soldier as any white boy. Well, they sure proved their point. We were some mighty thankful soldiers. One of the fellows said, "If I ever say any-

*Black Troops of K Company, 394th. (From "DAUNTLESS," p. 294. Permission: Taylor Publishing Company, Dallas, Texas.)*

thing bad about a black man again, you can slap me in the face." Well, we all felt the same way. And, by the way, we gave them all of the ammunition they wanted.

The official history of the 394th speaks of the colored troops, in these words, ". . . the colored platoon of K Co., which had already distinguished itself in its few days of battle, accounted for the major portion of the 300 POWs taken. . . ."

That night passed relatively quietly. Next morning our company, under Lt. Charles Gullette, was to go in a southeasterly direction and take the area just east of the city of Honningen. To do this we came down off the hill we were on. This proved difficult since it was covered with dense growth of all manner of things. Finally we got to the bottom of the hill, went across a field about 100 yards in width, and hit a road that ran into the town. We crossed this and a small stream and then climbed slowly up the hill we were to take. (See Map 3) We met no opposition, so we soon were at the top of this hill. Beyond we could see a forested area both to the south and east. To the west, between us and the city of Honningen, was another hilly area. As we looked around, we realized that we were very much alone. Lt. Gullette decided to take a break. He had us all eat lunch while he tried to figure out from the map just where we really were and what our next move should be.

In due time he said, "O.K., men, let's go." He started toward the woods to our south, but we did not go far at all. We hardly got up and started out than we came under heavy gun fire. How no one got hit, God alone knows. Of course, we all hit the dirt and tried to figure out where the firing was coming from. None of us could tell. After some time had gone by we tried moving again. Again we came under gun fire, and again no one was hit. We could not see where the shots were coming from, but we could tell from the way they were hitting that they were coming from woods to our east. Then we realized it was probably 20 mm cannon-type fire from a great distance. Someone was looking at us through a telescope and shooting at us only when we stood and moved because that was the only time they could really see us. So we decided to stay down and wait them out. Time went by. We all rested, ate what food we had left, and drank what water we had. At about 3:00 p.m. some guys were asking others for a drink of water because they had run out. But everyone had run out. And this was tough to take because we could all look down below and see the water running by in a stream. Finally one of the fellows said he could not take it any longer. He was going to make a run for it and get water. About 20 guys threw their canteens to him. He looped them all together, and tied them to his belt, and with a lunge took off down the hill, the canteens banging along behind him. But he did not make it more than 10 feet when bullets began hitting all around him. He turned around on a dime and came back and yelled out, "Fellows, I'm not thirsty any longer." He then proceeded to throw everyone's canteen back. We didn't blame him.

It got to be about 4:30. The Lt. was getting nervous. We had no radio, and if we did not make contact with our company or someone, we would not know the password and would be in big trouble. So he decided we had to leave the hill, go back the way we had come, and make contact. At his command we all got up and made a run for it. We ran down the hill toward the water. And nothing happened. We were mighty thankful. We figured that the gunners had left their area and were no longer eyeing us.

We were about three-fourths the way down the hill when all hell broke loose. We had jumped from the frying pan into the fire. Someone west of us, from town, was now shooting at us. We all hit the dirt and again tried to find where the fire was coming from. But we just could not see anyone. Finally we moved carefully, and fearfully, into a low spot. From this low spot we thought we could crawl to a higher spot and thus find out where the gunners were. Obviously they could see us at least when we were on higher ground. So one of the fellows moved out toward town. He was on his hands and knees. He had hardly gotten out of the low spot when bullets hit the ground in front of him and behind him. He did a regular jig, and it looked so funny that all of us laughed as if we were seeing the funniest act in town. Then a bullet hit his helmet and spun around inside his head liner, making a sound like a bee trying to sting him. This sent us into hysterics, as if we really were in a very funny situation. He fell back where he had started and gave us a free lecture to the effect that what was happening was not funny! What were we anyway, crazy? Well, I cannot explain our reaction to the situation. All I know was it all looked very funny and that we all laughed. Perhaps it was just a release of tension.

It was getting dark now, we had not gotten to the water yet, and we needed to make contact. The Lt. decided we just had to go forward, so again we just moved out, fearing the worst. But nothing happened. Perhaps the darkness protected us. We got to the stream and filled up our canteens. We had little pills we put into the water when we thought the water might be contaminated. We used them.

Now it was really dark. But the Lt. felt we only had

one course of action and that was to move out and make contact with our troops. So off we went. We got to the ditch that was beside the road and the Lt. had the guys get in the ditch. Then he sent me across the road and said that they would cover me. I took off in the darkness and got to about the middle of the road when a man who was obviously on guard called out, "Halt, who goes there?" Well, there I was, not knowing the password, and knowing that everyone was touchy since the Germans were making a good attempt at pushing us back across the Rhine. I looked behind me in the direction I realized he would be looking. I wanted to make sure I was not silhouetted. I wasn't. I then put my hands up to my mouth to make a megaphone effect, and instead of speaking towards him, spoke down the road. I said, "I don't know the pass. . ." Before I had said any more he started shooting. He shot to my left according to my deception. He shot all 8 of his shots from his M-1 and then jumped up and ran to the rear. He must not have been more than 25 or 30 feet from me. In the dark I could see him, since he was silhouetted. He had made me angry since I don't like to be shot at, and I had tried hard to speak in clear English, and he should have known I was no German. I yelled at him, "You dumb so and so. You are silhouetted and I could easily shoot you, but I won't. Get your officer and come back and talk."

At the shots, all of our fellows had taken off down the ditch. I walked right down the road and called out to them, Hey don't leave me behind, I'm O.K.," or something to that effect. I soon came up to them and reestablished contact. I told Hancock and the Lt. what was happening, and he came with me to where I had been before. About then an officer called out, "You still there?" We said, "Yes." He, out of the darkness, said, "Talk to me." The Lt. explained how we had been separated from everyone and because of that did not know the password of the day. He understood and told us where C Company was and that we were to go into town and meet them at a certain corner. We did not like it, but all walked right into town and up to the corner. But, no "C" Company. (Remember, this is all still in almost total darkness.) We knew that to stand there and wait would be suicide. So we just turned around and walked back. We could hear whistling and calls all around us. If the Germans thought we didn't know they were there they were wrong. We wondered if they would let us get all the way back out. We finally made it back. We told the officer our situation. He put us into a farmer's chicken houses which were all cleaned up and rather nice places, but small, and told us to get some rest. We thankfully did just that.

It seemed that only a minute went by and we were awakened. We were told that we were to go into town and take it before morning. It was now about 3:00 a.m. Street fighting. The thought was not very reassuring. We had all heard that it was difficult. But we knew the basics: (1) Don't ever stop moving. This way your enemy can never figure out where you are. (2) Don't let any soldiers remain in the homes along the route you take. If they are courageous, they will give you big trouble. So off we went. Sgt. Hancock was put in charge of half the men and I the other half. Lt. Gullette was in command. We each had about 15 or 20 men with us. We finally started toward town. We hardly had started when we heard, "Halt," in German. We all stayed still for a little while. The voice had come from well out in the field where we knew a machine gun was situated.

We had already decided to by-pass it if possible. When nothing happened we quietly went forward.

We moved up to the first houses that were right against the road. Another German called out, "Halt." This time from right in front of the Lieutenant. Crack, a shot went, and the German ran. The next few minutes we sweated blood, waiting to see what the Germans would do. They started to come back to their post but this time in force. The Lt. then quietly told us to pass the message back that he was going to throw a grenade and we would then go ahead if possible. He rolled the grenade down the street toward the Germans as they came up, and it went off right in the midst of them. We then all jumped up and charged the post and houses. I told the first two men behind me to go into the first home. Hancock was doing the same on the other side of the street. We had told the men they were to go into the houses, and as quickly as possible make sure no soldiers were in them. If they found no soldiers, they were to rejoin us as soon as possible. If they found soldiers, they were to take them prisoner and back to an agreed upon spot. We continued down the street, sending two soldiers as quickly as possible into every house. If the door would not open we just shot off the lock. Some homes had no soldiers in them, but many did.

Finally we came to the "T" in the road where we had been before. Turning around to talk to the man behind me, I found that no one was there. Later I found out that so many homes had had soldiers in them that our men had taken them prisoners and gone back with them, leaving us short handed. Therefore, we had to wait until they came back. We did not like it, since the first rule of street warfare is to keep moving. But we had to have men. Perhaps we should have gone back, but instead Lt. Gullette had us wait until all the men returned. We did hear movement in front of us and wondered who it could be. We thought it must be civilians. Later we realized it was German soldiers setting up their guns to stop our further advance. Finally all the men were back. Lt. Gullette passed back the message that we would go forward and down the right side of the "T" of the road. We just started when a machine gun opened up. I could see where the bullets were going since they had tracers in them. The tracers were necessary at night in order to tell the gunner where he was really shooting. They cut Lt. Gullette down, and I was sure I was next. I pulled in my gut, as if that would do any good.

The bullets never quite reached me. They hit the building across the street to my left and went off to one side. We, of course, hit the dirt, which in this case was the bottom of the gutter at the side of the street next to the sidewalk. Lt. Gullette was not dead and urged us to get the men shooting at us. I got up out of the gutter and joined Hancock on his side of the road, since the machine-gun bullets were coming from an area just to his left. Both Hancock and I looked around the corner of the building that had deflected the shots that otherwise would have hit me. We threw grenades, but to no apparent effect. Hancock and I tried to figure out what to do. We could see the tracers but could not tell where they came from. Throwing the grenades long or short did not seem to matter.

Then, I heard a metallic "ping" at my feet and a "potato masher" grenade went off. I felt a hot searing feeling several places on my legs and groin area and on my left hand. I knew I was in trouble. I told Hancock I was hit and was going back to the other side of the road and lie in the relative protection of the gutter and figure out how bad off I was. He agreed this was best. As I lay there in the road I realized that I was bleeding badly. I especially realized this when I almost passed out. But I could not tell how much damage the grenade had done. I wondered about Lt. Gullette, but he told me to forget him, he was done for. "Just get those Jerries."

Suddenly, Henry, one of our guys, began crying out, "This is it. This is it." I told him to shut up and the Germans would think they killed us all and we could crawl back and get out of this mess. He kept yelling, "But this is it. This is it." At the time I could not figure out what he was talking about. But later I realized that he was talking about his dream—the dream he had told us on the truck ride to Remagen. At that time he had said he had a dream that we would go down a valley and into a town at night and all be killed. Suddenly, he got up and ran. He was immediately shot down. His "god" had not really given him good information, since the rest of us managed to crawl out of the mess.

Both Hancock and I realized we had to get out of the street before dawn or we would all be killed, since our enemy now knew where we were. So we told a few fellows to go back and find a house, capture it, and we would all get to it and defend it as best we could with the men we had. We gave, I believe, Meehan and a few others about 15 minutes to take this action. We later found out they had gone back and had seen a large home up the side of a rise with space around it, ideal for defense. They had gone up to the door but found it closed and locked. They had backed off and shot a bazooka round at the door in order to get in, but just at that moment the lady of the house opened the door. The shell went into the house, in some way missing her, and hit her great big kitchen stove, went off, and made a great big hole in it. She was furious, and told the fellows just what she thought of them. They, of course, shoved her aside, took over, and told her to please shut up, that after all there was a war going on.

After waiting about 15 minutes and getting more and more nervous because it was beginning to get light, we all moved back, crawling along in the gutter since it happened to be deep enough that it afforded us protection from the machine gunner who had to shoot at an angle, thus able to shoot above the side-walk but not below sidewalk level. After I had gone perhaps 100 feet in this way I got up and walked back down the street wondering if I was going to pass out and how I would know which house the fellows had taken. A voice out of the dark said, *"Hans, dass du?"* In English: "Hans, is that you?" "Ja, Ja," I answered and kept right on going. I am sure it was a German soldier, but did not think that it was the time to get into a shoot-out.

Going just a little farther, one of the fellows suddenly appeared and pointed to the house. It had now become light enough to dimly see perhaps 20 or 30 feet. I went into the house and lay down on a couch in the front room. The woman of the house was still fuming mad, and one of the fellows explained why. We asked her to please shut up. Finally three or four of us wounded were in the front room while the rest of the fellows had gone outside and taken up defensive positions. But the Germans had come to realize what had happened and so started shooting at the fellows as they took their positions. Also someone with a fairly large caliber gun was shooting at the house. The bullets were going through the walls, and if any of us had been standing, we might well have been killed. We realized we had to get down in the cellar if we were to survive. We did so, the minute we could. But the German lady was getting on our nerves. One of the fellows who could speak some German told her, "Look lady, this is war. We are sorry we shot up your stove. But either you shut up and help us by getting us food and water or we are going to have to tie you up, tape your mouth, and put you where you will be out of our way."

Just like that her whole behavior changed. From then on we had one of the nicest hostesses you ever did see. I remember she brought me water and some delicious sausages. It was about then that the Germans began really shooting things up, and Meehan came running in to say that if the Germans charged the house, he doubted we could hold it. At this time he noticed that he had blood on his boots. He pulled up his pant leg and found that a bullet had gone through the muscle part of his lower leg and that he had not even noticed it. He was not bleeding much and said he was going back out to help defend the place. Some of us said we would do what we could to help. He had hardly left when he came back and said our tanks were now coming up the road, the same road we had so recently come up. He said, "You ought to see it. The Germans are standing out in the road where we were and are shooting at the tanks with just their rifles. The tankers are mowing them down."

Hardly any time at all went by and soldiers who were with the tanks came in and told us that they would take over. In perhaps half an hour I was taken out on a stretcher, put on a jeep, and driven off down a road along the Rhine. Soon we went by the Remagen Bridge. I asked why they did not use it. They said it was about to collapse. It did later that day. Besides that, the engineers had put in a pontoon bridge we would use. Sure enough, we came to a bridge made of floating units all attached together with cables at angles attached to the pontoons and to shore. The road part of the pontoon bridge was hardly 12 inches above the rushing water. The Rhine is a very fast-moving river at this point. It seemed impossible that the engineers could have put in such a bridge so quickly. Big stuff was crossing both ways and groups were having to take turns, since the bridge was only wide enough for a single lane of traffic. A group of us wounded were taken across to a field hospital on the west side of the Rhine. A doctor looked me over and took a few pieces of metal out of my legs and looked over my left hand, especially my index finger which had really been ripped up. He bandaged me up and said I would be okay in due time, but he thought I should be evacuated so I would not reopen the wounds and possibly bleed to death. I cannot say that I was unhappy to hear this. The date was March 17, St. Patrick's Day. The next day we were flown in a DC-3 to Paris from a makeshift grass airport next to the field hospital. It was my first plane ride, and I thoroughly enjoyed it.

## PARIS, FRANCE
## MARCH 18-22, 1945

I wrote home on March 19:
**"I am at the present time, taking a little vacation in Paris because of a wound I received. It isn't very**

bad. I am what they call walking wounded. I suppose you received a telegram saying the same. I sure hope it did not scare you or anything. They brought me here by plane. My first ride was really O.K. We got to see all the country we had been fighting over from a little different angle. The country was pretty nice looking, but Germany was full of bomb craters and ruined buildings. No country has begun to suffer from bombing like Germany has. - I'm awful sorry I couldn't write, but we were moving so fast when we went from the Erft Canal to the Rhine that there just wasn't time, and besides that they wouldn't take mail."

My parents were notified of my situation. A postal card came to them saying, "I am pleased to inform you that on March 24, 1945, your son, S/Sgt. William F. McMurdie, 39294352, was MAKING NORMAL IMPROVEMENT. Diagnosis, Lacerated wound of corona. Very truly yours, B. M. Welion, Capt."

My parents thought this meant I had been hit in the eye, but this was not the case. It was just in a very delicate part of the body, along with all the lacerations here and there. It was several weeks before the last pieces of metal worked their way to the surface and were pulled out.

While in the hospital in Paris I wrote on March 20 to Art Ude. In answer to a question of his I wrote:
"I have never carried my gas mask yet while in combat. As soon as we hit the front lines they take them away from us. Yes, we had the new ones. I haven't seen one for so long, though, that I can't remember

too much about them." (I include this as part of the historical record and am puzzled as to why the officials felt gas masks were not needed. It is of course true that during World War II gas was not used by either side as far as I know.)

## HOSPITAL IN ENGLAND
## MARCH 22-MAY 8, 1945

March 23: Dear Mom and Dad,
"I took another plane ride, and now I'm somewhere in England. The trip was a little bumpier than the first. It felt like I was on a fishing boat on a rough day. . . . The doc said that everything is O.K. and that in time I'd be as good as new. I was glad to hear that." On the 24th I wrote: "Yesterday we had a visit from 5 little English girls. One of the boys tried to teach them a song to the tune of 'Mares Eat Oats'. It went:
> '88s and Hand Grenades, and lots of
> screaming meemies I'd jump in a hole
> too, wouldn't you?'"

They could not understand what was meant by screaming meemies, although we did try to explain that they were a type of artillery shell that made a screaming noise as they went by.

On the 28th I wrote:
"Today's news sure does sound good. I sort of wish I was up there with the rest of the guys now, but I guess I'll get back soon enough." On the 30th: "Things are still coming along O.K. I've been playing chess with one of the boys here. He is a little

better than I, so I'm learning a little." On April 5: "I'm still in England here at the hospital, and doing O.K. I got awful tired of the ward so I took a walk around the whole place. There are the usual number of German prisoners working around. One of them spoke English rather well. He called his guard 'Sir,' and asked permission to go after some equipment. I wonder where he was educated." On the 7th: "Today was just like any other of these hospital days, except for one thing; they handed me a Purple Heart. It really is a very beautiful medal. I sent it home along with some other ribbons I have received at one time or another." On the 9th: "Another fellow and I went to Church Sunday. They sang 'Holy, Holy, Holy'; and all I could think of was our church back there in Pasadena. The Chaplain preached a good sermon on a subject that you could call, 'Without God and His teachings, there will never be a lasting peace.' He missed saying; 'That is, with trust in Christ at all times, . . . I was just thinking about things we saw in Germany. What impressed me was that in many cellars you would find a big pile of coal, and right beside it a big pile of potatoes. Also the canned, or rather bottled apple sauce, cherries, etc.; and then the hams and bacon in a cooler. Also every cellar seemed to have the same cement roof supported by many poles, with the cellar itself being the actual living quarter of the family; stove, beds, or at least mattresses, and anything else they needed. I guess they were well prepared."

Reading through the letters I sent home I notice that I discuss the fact that I was trying to figure out what to do with my life, and could not come to any conclusion. I also notice that although I would touch on my war experiences, I just could not write about them at length. So my parents asked me about my being wounded and I wrote:

**"I think that map was correct. I was wounded in the city of Honningen. It has been 2 weeks since it happened, so it is O.K. to tell you. We went over the bridge that day after the first boys went across. I guess that ought to be enough on that subject."** And then I go on to other subjects.

An inability to talk about the war experiences continued until rather recently. I remember being asked by Rev. George Orviek, the President of the Evangelical Lutheran Synod, about my experiences. This was some time in the 1980s. I did tell him a few things that happened. But as I spoke I re-lived the events. It was so upsetting that I just felt it best not to talk again about what happened. I have noticed this is true of most of the fellows I have met who have seen actual combat. I remember a man in a congregation I served who came back from Korea and absolutely refused to talk about what he had gone through. For some reason I can now talk about these things. Why, I really don't know. I do notice that when I speak of the events I do not re-live the event with all of its horrors. It is more as if I were talking about a book I have read.

On April 15, in reference to the Battle of the Bulge, I wrote,

**"Yes, the Germans got my Bible and everything else: razor, straps, underwear, swimming trunks, map of England - all marked off where I had traveled, sleeping bag, a swell axe, shoes, everything."**

I did not tell them how I also experienced a feeling of being violated, and terribly mistreated. At first I thought that perhaps I felt as I did because these physical things had come to mean too much to me. But I have come to believe that there is more to it than that. I believe we each have a deep inner sense of right and wrong, and when we are wronged this sense of having been personally violated or wronged can be quite overwhelming. But I also have noticed that since that experience of losing all the material things I owned, material things have not meant much to me.

In that letter of April 15, I also said,
**"I'm reading a book now I'm really enjoying. It is Brave Men by Ernie Pyle. If you want to read the real dope, read that book. David Copperfield came to a happy ending yesterday."** In a letter of the 17th I again mention that I was reading *Brave Men*. I then write, **"Well, the fellows have started to fight the war over again, so I'll listen in. But for me there is always the why of it all."**

On the 20th:
**"I'm still doing O.K. Today I played Basketball for two hours and really wore myself out. . . . A Red Cross Club mobile came here today. They gave out donuts and coffee as usual. I'm afraid the donuts ruined my supper, because I sure didn't eat much."** 22nd of April: **"Yesterday morning I visited Bristol for about 1/2 hour. We were just driving through. The country here is really marvelous. Almost any spot looks like a gallery painting. I see Mr. Churchill was in town the same day as we were. I'm afraid I missed him. . . . We went to the show the other day with an English radio technician. We saw Donald O'Conner**

and Peggy O'Brian in 'Patrick the Great.' We all enjoyed it a lot. There were some Colored boys in Royal Air Force uniforms, so we asked the Englishman about them. He said they were from Jamaica or colonies in Africa. It was the first colored English troops that I'd seen in England."

At the end of April I talk about a 3-day pass in London, and then a 7-day visit to Scotland. In Scotland we visited Robert Burns country and the Clyde. "The country all around here is the most beautiful I've ever seen. The rolling hills with many colored trees and an occasional lush green meadow really is just made for a picture. The streams are crystal clear, flowing over beautiful rock formations which are shaded by many graceful trees." I went on to both Glasgow and Edinburgh, but must not fill these pages with all the information I wrote home. The most memorable event was meeting a Scotsman on the bus and trying to talk to him. I could not understand what he was trying to say. Later I met him fishing for salmon on the river that runs out of Loch Lomond to the Clyde. He gave me the rod and reel and showed me how to use them, but his rig was of a type new to me and I could not handle it. I think he got a little disgusted with me. I thanked him and walked on up to see the lake. I was surprised at how large it was and surrounded by low mountains.

In a letter written May 2: "I've just been reading in the English papers about all the atrocities and have been to a show to see if they would show everything, and brother, they really have shown the British everything. I think now, more than ever before, the people of England, and I guess America, know what we have been fighting for. Just to think that the

Nazi would have done anything like they did is bad enough, but to come as close to it as the English did is really something. When you talk to them about it they say it was an act of God that saved them. They knew that they couldn't have kept Hitler out. You would be very surprised at how little it takes to conquer an unprepared people. . . . I can't seem to get anything for Mother's Day, so remember that you still are the swellest, greatest, Mom a guy could have, so you had better take care of yourself and not worry about me. If there is anything you see around that you want, just get it and ask Dad for the money. (He can get it out of my bank account.)"**

On May 4, I was told I was to go back to my old outfit which was still on the battle line. I did not look forward to going back. In fact, I dreaded it, even though I could see that the war was almost over. In a V-Mail dated May 6: **"From the way the English act you can tell one thing. They are very much relieved that the Germans have been crushed."**

A group of us were taken to Southampton to be shipped back to our outfits. On May 8th we were standing on the dock ready to get aboard the ship. Then suddenly the ship's horn blew a great blast and the words, "Now hear this! Now hear this! The war in Europe is over. The Captain invites everyone to come aboard and have steak with him. Or you can go back to the barracks. Because of the war's end, we will not be leaving here for a few days." That was truly good news. I was greatly relieved and thankful to God for the end of the war.

General Van Fleet sent the following letter to our General Lauer. I include it since it gives you an overview of our Divisions activities from March 9th to the end of the War on May 8th.

HEADQUARTERS III CORPS
Office of the Commanding General
APO 303, U.S. Army

11 May 1945

Major General Walter E. Lauer,
Commanding General, 99th Infantry Division,
APO 99, U.S. Army

My dear General Lauer:

Victory in Europe is here and the military operation of the fighting 99th Division against the German Army are at end. It is fitting at this time that I express my feelings of admiration and gratitude to you and your splendid Division for the magnificent work you have done. Your operations will stand out as a brilliant page in the history of the Western Front.

On 9th March 1945, two days after the seizure of the Remagen bridgehead, and at a time when the enemy had strongly reacted to the Rhine crossing, the 99th Division was attached to the III Corps. On 10 March it entered the bridgehead and assumed command of a zone four miles in width. Despite extremely rugged terrain, a wide zone of advance and a strong enemy resistance, the Division attacked relentlessly and gained objectives, thus contributing materially to the rapid expansion of the bridgehead.

Between 23-25 March the Division attacked and advanced more than four miles through difficult terrain and strong enemy resistance, catching the enemy by surprise. This advance made it possible for the 7th Armored Division to break through and make its sensational 130 mile drive to WETZLAR, GIESSEN and the EDERSTAU-SEE.

Following the breakthrough, the division by skillful use of motors, advanced rapidly behind the 7th Armored Division, moving approximately 110 air miles and captured 3,859 prisoners of war during the period 25-30 March.

Between 5-17 April the division attacked the Ruhr pocket in a zone four and one-half miles wide and through almost impassable terrain. Despite precipitous mountains and strong enemy resistance, through the indomitable spirit of the 99th Division, it covered approximately 40 air line miles and captured 37,968 prisoners of war.

After the liquidation of the Ruhr pocket, the division proceeded to the Third Army zone, where it attacked southeast, and between 24 April and 2 May drove 75 air line miles to the southeast. During this time the division crossed the ALTMUHL, DONAU AND ISAR rivers and took 15,455 prisoners of war.

From 11 March until 2 May the 99th Division was attacking almost continuously. Its brilliant successes were in a large measure a result of the determined, aggressive spirit of the troops and of your sound leadership.

I look forward with great pleasure to further associations with your grand division. All are proud of you.

Sincerely,

J.A. VAN FLEET
Major General, U.S. Army Commanding

## BACK TO THE 99TH DIVISION
## MAY 10-22, 1945

In due time we got aboard ships to return to our outfits. In my letter of the 12th: **"I'm now in a place in France that is 18 miles south of the city of Luxembourg. The trip from Southampton to Le Havre was made at night while I was sleeping. The sea was as calm as it could be, so no one got sea sick. We came from the 10th Replacement Depot which is between Birmingham and Litchfield, England, by train through London to Southampton. At Le Havre we got on a train and went through a lot of places and then to here, which is the 14th Replacement Depot. I counted up my points for discharge."**

That the war was ending had been clear for some time. So a debate had developed over how it would be decided who was going to be discharged first, and on what basis, etc. A point system was set up. So many points for months of service, so many added points for months served overseas, so many points for each battle you had been in, so many points for medals won, so many points for each child you had, etc. I had not served long and was not married, so had only 55 points. It was obvious I would be in Europe for a while yet.

Also in the letter of May 12: **"Well, all Japan has to do is quit and I'll be satisfied."**

We all realized that there still was a job to do before the war was really over. And many of us were going to have to go over there and get the job done. About this time I received the following (recall that our outfit was "A" Company, 394th Infantry Regiment, therefore part of the First Battalion which was made up of Companies A,B,C,D plus attached units):

HEADQUARTERS 99TH INFANTRY DIVISION APO 449 United States Army

5 May 1945

(GENERAL ORDERS)

NUMBER 35

BATTLE HONORS - FIRST BATTALION THREE NINETY FOURTH INFANTRY
Under the provisions of Section IV War Department Circular 333 (1943) and Section III, Circular 6, Headquarters Third United States Army, dated 26 April 1944, citation of the following unit, as approved by the Commanding General, First United States Army, is announced. The citation reads as follows:

The First Battalion, Three Ninety Fourth Infantry Regiment, is cited for outstanding performance of duty in action against the enemy during the period 16 to 18 December 1944, in Germany and Belgium. The German's Ardennes offensive was spearheaded directly at the First Battalion, Three Ninety Fourth Infantry Regiment, which was defending a front of three thousand five hundred yards and protecting the right flank of the Ninety Ninth Infantry Division. The enemy launched its initial attack against the First Battalion with an unprecedented artillery concentration lasting approximately two hours, followed by an attack of six battalions of infantry, supported by tanks, dive bombers, flame throwers, and rockets. For two days and nights the battalion was under intensive small arms fire and continuous artillery concentrations, with little food and water, and no hope of replenishing a rapidly dwindling supply of ammunition. Knowing that reserves were unavailable, the men of this battalion, with indomitable spirit and confidence, repeatedly beat back the superior numbers of the enemy forces coming at them from the front, flanks, and rear. Many times the men rose out of their foxholes to meet the enemy in fierce hand-to-hand combat. Outnumbered six to one they inflicted extremely heavy casualties upon the enemy. By their tenacious stand, the First Battalion, Three Ninety Fourth Infantry Regiment, prevented the enemy from penetrating the right flank of an adjacent division, and permitted other friendly forces to reinforce the sector. The unflinching courage and devotion to duty displayed by the officers and men of the First Battalion, Three Ninety Fourth Infantry Regiment, and in the face of overwhelming odds was in keeping with the highest traditions of the military service.

The First Battalion, Three Ninety Fourth Infantry Regiment, is entitled to the citation streamer. The individuals assigned or attached to this unit on the occasion for which citation was awarded are entitled to wear the Distinguished Unit Badge. Individuals subsequently assigned or attached are entitled to wear the Distinguished Unit Badge only as long as they remain with the unit.

BY COMMAND OF MAJOR GENERAL LAUER: OFFICIAL:

R. B. WARREN
Colonel, GSC
Chief of Staff

JOHN R. ACHOR
Lieutenant Colonel, AGD
Adjutant General

The wording above is a little flowery and perhaps gives us more credit than is due. I never saw nor talked to any of our fellows about any hand-to-hand combat. I am not saying it did not happen, but it surely was not general. Also I should perhaps point out that I have limited what I said to what I personally directly saw or took part in. I have not told about things the fellows recounted, since I thought this would then just get too long. Perhaps I should say one particular thing about our company. We had several Jewish fellows in our outfit. One of them was one of our first casualties. I mention this since even while serving in the Army I had men tell me several times that the Jewish fellows got all of the nice soft jobs way back of the front lines.

On May 22 I report that we are still at the replacement depot, and living in 8-man tents, sleeping on cots: Also, **"I met a fellow from our platoon today. He was a** replacement who got his feet frost bitten while we were up front near Eisenborn. He remembered me. He was there from January 2 to 25."** (Many do not realize that in combat your biggest fight is often just keeping physically healthy.)

In a letter dated May 26, I write, **"Well all seems to be coming along O.K. I'm still getting boils though."** I believe I got boils because we did not pay close attention to keeping clean. When we were in training this was greatly stressed. However on the battle field this was not stressed, and I believe our burning gasoline for heat and light in our holes was a bad idea. I am sure we would have all griped if the officers had made an issue of keeping clean, but I think it would have been best if they had.

On May 27, I write: **"Who would have thought that I ever would be in Nuremberg, Germany, or rather about 10 miles east of it? We are in the 90th Reinforcement Battalion, waiting transportation to our outfits."** Then I tell about the train trip to the Nuremberg area. **"The marshalling yards, every one we went through, every railroad car was a twisted mass of wreckage, as were the surrounding few buildings, and factories. The railroad cars were often burned so that all that remained was the wheels and the main steel members. You never saw such a yard of skeletons as we saw at every town on the way - Metz, Mainz, Stuttgart, Frankfort on Main, Brandanberg, Nuremberg and every town and city between. Sometimes the rails and ties would be standing straight up into the air, or maybe curled back like a potato peeling. . . . The main cities are just brick rubble, with an occasional part of a building in livable con-

**ditions."**

I then mention the names of few towns which were not so badly hit and how we made our train trip in "40 and 8" cars. What is meant is a freight car that could hold 40 people or 8 cattle. I then tell that, **"The rails are jammed with trains going both ways. We passed, going the other way, an average of 10 trains during daylight, filled with French, Belgian, Dutch, German, civilians or soldiers. We always cheered the French, etc., and just gave the Germans a dirty look. We figured an average of 2,000 aboard every one of those trains. Out of ten trains, 7 would be French, 2 Belgian, 1 German - mostly soldiers who were turned loose by the Russians upon capture unless they are SS. You never saw anything like it. The whole of Europe seems to be moving, going back home. You could tell the Germans had only taken the best (for slave labor). These people were all strong and healthy looking, even after what they had been through. A train stopped besides us and one of the Belgian soldiers who had been captured 2 years ago spoke to us in English. He had been liberated by the Russians. He said, 'the Russians are equipped almost entirely with American trucks, tanks, and big equipment....' He explained most of the fellows in the train he was on had been doing work in Berlin, pencil pushing, before that as a factory worker. He said food (at end of war) was 3 potatoes, 1 piece of bread, some soup as a day's ration."**

We had traveled 360 miles in 90 hours, or 4 miles per hour, average. A Belgian soldier said it was 100 meters forward, a 2 hour stop, etc., but then he said, **"We are free!"** I comment: **"You ought to get a look at these**

Germans. They look at us with solemn faces. If I ever saw a beaten look, it is the ones they have. . . . Germans are walking the roads, hooking rides all over, trying to get home. Lots of them are in uniform. It seems funny not to shoot at them, but we aren't armed so we can't anyway. . . . At the present time we are living in German barracks, in the lap of luxury - showers, beds with springs, big day rooms, all in four story brick buildings. It is strictly all right. . . "

## MARKTHEIDENFELD, GERMANY
### May 29-July 9, 1945

May 29, 1945: Dear Mom and Dad,
"I'm back at the Company now. The platoon has 53 men in it, where there is only supposed to be 40. You can see that things are lots different. The Lieutenant, Dodd, is a swell fellow. He came the day after V-E day. We never did have a Lieutenant in actual combat. The fellows say that Honningen was the worst combat that we were ever in. After that it was just a forced march. They even admitted that it was easier than from the Erft Canal to the Rhine, which I thought was pretty easy. The name of the place we are in is Marktheidenfeld, with the Main River about 150 yards away. . . . Wurzberg is where our Division Headquarters is at, about 25 miles away. We had a beautiful truck drive back up here. The Germans are all out tilling the soil, and tending their crops. It doesn't look as if they would starve. - We are living in one barracks of a group of about 10 barracks that was used to house people who had been bombed out. They are all very nice. German prisoners are in the

other barracks. We put guards on them and take care of them as to what they do, otherwise they do everything for themselves. They eat captured rations and do their own cooking. On the whole they don't look too healthy. Some of the fellows are 16 years old, but some look like they are only 12. There are about 250 here now, 250 more are expected. We will have a time keeping them all busy. - I was surprised to see how much they use rivers and streams for transportation. The Main is full of sunken barges and boats. The Rhine was the same. - You ought to see Wurzberg. It is the flattest town I've seen. Not a building standing in the city, just a wall or two. The Service Company couldn't find any whole buildings so they have to live in big German trailers. . . . So long, Bill"

In a letter dated May 30, 1945, from Marktheidenfeld, mention is made of a German medical captain who spoke excellent English, and that he had not heard from the outside world since the war started and he wanted to know about this penicillin that the fellows were talking about. One of the fellows said it was really good stuff. It could cure gonorrhea in 5 shots. The doctor "almost collapsed." Mention is made of Mings being back. He had had trench foot. (My parents had asked if it were true that on January 1, 1945 I had been the only one left in my original squad that had gone

Teenage POWs

overseas.) I answer, **"Yes, when I became Sergeant we got 11 replacements, all fresh from the States."** (But you note that all had not been killed, since so many got trench foot or frost bite.) I also write, **"We found out that a lot of our boys were taken prisoner, not killed, in the Bulge. . . . The boys are telling me how they came to a place where they could see the Alps on one side and the Carpathians on the other. They sure were glad they didn't have to climb those mountains. Italy surrendered so they were told to hold fast. . . . That Castle in the picture was at St. Pierre about 3 miles North of Aubel, Belgium. It is also near that big American cemetery that was in Life Magazine. I saw it. Didn't make me feel good. I know more than one guy that is probably there."**

In a letter dated June 2, **"Yes, anyone that is wounded by enemy action gets the Purple Heart. Yes, I am still getting boils. They sure are a pest."** June 4: **"If we stay here it will really be all right. They are very lenient with us. I am Platoon Special Service. My job is to make sure the German prisoners go to work outside the camp, and that they get to their work and are fed. . . . I am glad you realize that I will not get home right away."** June 5: **"I was talking to a German Lieutenant this morning. About all he could say was that 90 million Germans needed more land. He said Hitler was mad, thinking he could conquer the world, but he saw nothing wrong with taking Poland, Austria, etc. . . ."**

"We need more land" was one of Hitler's main arguments for conquest.

June 9: "[Germans say] **'I see that you are moving equipment up to the Russian front. I suppose you will** start fighting them soon.' One thing the Germans said over and over again was that we were surely now going to fight Russia. We said, 'No, we are not going to fight the Russians'. The Germans always acted amazed when we told them this." June 11: "We have had no trouble with any Germans yet."

In this same letter I tell of the different vehicles that we were using transporting the prisoners to work. Why we did not have U.S. trucks, I do not know. We were using German and Italian trucks and had a lot of trouble keeping them going. One truck was run by using wood chips as fuel. It was tricky to operate, since what went to the engine were the gases from the partially burned wood chips, and it was tricky to keep the chips burning and having the fumes go through the cleaning device and then into the regular engine. (It would be somewhat like the engines now being run off natural gas.) The trouble was that the fire would go down, so we would not get enough fumes to keep going until we pulled off the road for a while and got the fire going again. The furnace part that finished the "gas" looked like a super-large water heater behind the cab.

Rather than continue to quote from letters, I'll mention a few things, quoting when it seems appropriate. We were taking prisoners out to help the farmers with their crops and I note: **"Haven't seen a tractor yet, just cows, oxen, and horses (being used to pull plows, etc.)"** On June 14: **"Today we went out into the woods with some boys to get a little lumber to build sentry towers. These kids are from 15-17."** In the same letter mention is made of the tremendous amount of equipment which was moving through Marktheidenfeld, over the bridge that crosses the Main River at that point, on to a storage area. The Germans could not believe that we had so much equipment. They were sure we were driving it around in circles to impress them.

June 15: **"They are catching pretty good fish in the Main these days. The fish seem to bite best about 1/2 hour before sundown.... Today I took some Germans out to do some work on a farm 14 miles from here. We went south along the Main for about 8 miles, and then inland along a valley with wooded hills on both sides. Bavaria seems to be a beautiful part of Germany."** June 18 records hauling chow to Karlstad and picking up gravel to repair roads in our area. **"Some boys are out of money and wanted me to contribute to the cause. I asked, 'What cause?' They said, 'Cause we ain't got none.'"** I did not contribute. June 22: **"Today I took some of our POWs out to work at a bed factory. The big boss can speak English and his superintendent is an American."** A newspaper clipping dated June 26 records, **"85ers Trickling Home From ETO."** June 28: **"We are still here and doing the same old stuff.... Today two other fellows and I took a trip to Affshaffenberg, or however you spell it."** June 29: **"Who do you think came up today? None other than Happy, Clark Cavett. I sure was glad to see him."** June 30: **"How do you like our new stationery?"**

July 1, 1945: **"WACS, 35 of them, came up to A Company and threw a party, and what a party. Whiskey and wine galore, so a lot of guys were drunk. It really was a mess."** July 3: **"We haven't had any trouble with the Germans yet, but we have heard about it. Affshaffenberg is a Nazi stronghold. They fought to the end there, and the 393rd says they are** looking and trying to find out where they are holding reported meetings." July 4: "We have every bridge guarded. The boys search every vehicle and make sure the Germans show their passes and other papers, then they can go across. Outside certain towns we have check points. All Jerries are checked there. Other fellows stand guard at the billets or Command Post. We have others that go out with the details, to watch the prisoners. Five men go to the bed factory, others with the road details."

The main thing I remember about those days is taking a group of men out with gravel and road tar and leaving them off somewhere with a few guards. The German prisoners then used the materials to repair the roads. I also remember the visits to the bed factory since the prisoners were working alongside civilians, and the German fellow that owned the factory spoke English and liked to talk to us. He sometimes needed gasoline in order to do some business and we could sometimes manage to get him some, which he greatly appreciated.

## NEUENDETTELSAU, GERMANY
### July 10-August 1, 1945

Some of you who know a little history of the Lutheran Church will realize that this is the city of Rev. William Loehe, a German pastor who sent many men to America to help build up the Christian Church in America. In his book, *A History of the Christian Church,* Qualben says, "An outstanding missionary leader was Rev. William Loehe of Neuendettelsau in Bavaria, who was instrumental in sending about sixty trained workers into the new settlements (of America). In addition, he sent about fifty students to the seminary of the newly organized Missouri Synod" (p. 489). Even though I had been brought up in the Missouri Synod, I had not heard of this man but did later when I was at seminary.

July 10: "I am now with 'C' Company, 26th Infantry Regiment of the 1st Division. It looks like we are in for occupation."

What was happening was that men were being moved around on the basis of the points they had so that a unit would be made up of men within a certain number of points. And then they would be shipped home. This of course broke up the group with which I had fought, since men had different numbers of points depending on length of service, etc., as noted previously.

July 12: "I am now Squad leader of the 3rd Squad of the 2nd Platoon of C Company, 26th Infantry, 1st Division, 3rd Army. That ought to be perfectly clear. At present we are guarding a P. W. cage with about 1,000 Germans, SS and Wehrmacht mixed. One got away last week. The prisoners live in an airplane repair depot. Engines and parts are all over the woods where we are located. The depot is well camouflaged, being deep in the woods like it is. July 18: "I found out that the town that the company is in is 100% Lutheran . . . It is one of the best looking and nicest small towns I've seen." July 22: "Today they asked the Squad Leaders to write articles on Combat Experiences for the War Department. They gave me the topic of *CLOTHING AND EQUIPMENT*. I wrote on the overcoat and gloves in the winter time." I wrote what I have previously written, namely that once the overcoats got wet, and the temperature went below freezing, they froze solid in the shape they were in, and thus became useless.

On July 26 I wrote that it was nice to hear that Burke Gill was now a Brigadier General. He was a relative on my dad's side of the family. I was also trying to teach myself how to type, and was using a German typewriter. I noted that the SS insignia was on one of the keys, looking like two bolts of lightening, and then struck the key a number of times as example.

July 31: **"Pastor Niemoller said, 'The German people are very different. They like to be governed; they like to feel authority.' I think he is right. The Germans even like to work for the Americans, and they always do a good job.** (Pastor Niemoller was a famous Lutheran pastor who resisted Hitler.) . . . **We are supposed to go to Nuremberg soon. Our Battalion is going to do all the M. P. duty, guarding P. W's, installations, and maybe the trials. Well, someone said 'chow.' . . . Bill"** August 1: **"We did little today except turned in our helmet liners. They are going to put an MP on it. It seems that our Platoon is to do MP duty in Nuremberg. Who thought that it would ever come to this?"**

General Lauer in his book *Battle Babies* recounts our occupation duties, and then explains why we were being transferred from one outfit to another, and why I suddenly was transferred from the 99th Division to the 1st Division, etc. I include a little he says about occupation duties, since it gives a little background to what I experienced. He writes, in part (pp. 323-331):

"Combat was over, and now occupation duties confront the Division. Forty-eight hours after the 'Unconditional Surrender,' the 'Battle Babies' rolled into the Main-Franken area to which they were assigned for occupational duties. . . . The Main River flows across it from east to west. The district is mostly agricultural. The main industrial towns are Wurzburg, the capital, and Schweinfurt, the center of the roller-bearing works. . . .

"Then began the task of establishing law and order and civil government. . .Thousands upon thousands of German soldiers were processed through the great discharge center we established at Ochsenfurt. As quickly as their identity was established by our prisoner of war interrogation teams and it was determined that they were not among those wanted for war crimes, they were given a discharge and identification paper and returned to their home towns or close enough thereto so that they could walk home. Their manpower was needed by the local Burgermeisters, and we did all we could to release this horde of men to make their manpower available to the local authorities. These ex-soldiers, almost without exception, wanted only to get home, find their families, shed their uniforms, and go to work. . . .

"For our fighting men, relief that the war was over was mingled with the uncertainty of the future. What was to happen next? How long were they to stay in occupation? Would they be re-deployed to the Pacific Theater of Operations? Would they go home? The war in the Pacific had not stopped. . . .Then began the insistent clamor of the folks at home to bring the soldiers back and disband the army. . . . Finally it was announced that certain units had been selected to be returned to the

United States for demobilization, among which was the 99th Infantry Division. At the same time an "adjusted service rating" (A.S.R.), a "point system," was published for the selection of men as individuals, to be returned to the United States with these selected units for discharge. . . . Points! - Points! - POINTS! - the bane of a soldier's existence from then on. The low point personnel in the 99th Division were parceled out to units remaining in Europe, and the Division received the high point men from these organizations. Soon the 99th Division contained men from almost every organization in the European Theater of Operations, and it received its embarkation orders.

"It was the end of the 'Battle Babies,' the end of many deep friendships - comradeships. . . . On 24 Sept.1945 it arrived in the United States and at Norfolk, Va., and at Camp Miles Standish, Mass., (from which point it had set sail for Europe), and was inactivated 27 Sept. 1945."

### MP—FURTH, GERMANY
### August 2-September 14, 1945

August 2: Dear Mom and Dad, **"I am now Charge of Quarters in our temporary billets on the Tumstrasse in Furth. We have MP on our helmets and a lot of law to lay down. I guess that we will start tomorrow. Furth is about 5 miles North of Nuremberg, but the two cities touch. . . . We came here from Neuendetteslau in German trucks. I don't know why. Some of the guys are guarding the Farben Chemical Works."** I then go on to describe the confusion of our outfit moving in and the other outfit moving out.

August 4: "Well, it looks like it will be a long time before any of us get home. The War had better end soon, because I'm just plain tired of being in the Army.... Two of my men got shot up last night. A guard halted them, and they didn't halt. 10% beer had taken effect. One shot was fired and hit one fellow in the hand and leg, and the other in the leg. They will be in the hospital a while I'm afraid."

Things had been very lax since the end of the war, and had really gotten out of hand. General Patton was trying to shape the men up, since one result of the laxness was that unnecessary accidents were taking place. Another was that raids were being made on people who were suspected of doing something wrong. The trouble was that our men took whatever they wished. So I commented in a letter, "All I call them are legalized looting patrols. What always gets me is how these civilian chore women that clean up our rooms never take a thing. I often have an orange laying on the table. Not one has gone, and none of the other fellows have missed a thing."

In a letter to my sister, dated August 8, I again talk about looting and mention that the pen I was using I had taken from a dead German soldier. I thought you would be interested in what I wrote: "I always figured that what I took from a dead German was mine, and what I could have taken from a live German was his, and it was best he kept it.... Some fellows made it a business of taking anything the German soldiers had. I know one fellow that has made several thousand dollars selling this stuff he has looted. (I just wanted to show you that the U.S. is no angel when it comes to unlawful things.) Every time I read an article picturing the G. I. as an angel and the Germans as Devils and Beasts I just burn up with the thought of how ignorant civilians are about what actually happens over here." I then write, "I've been reading all about this new bomb, and am hoping that it will end the war very soon. I sure would like to see things come to an end without any more D-Days." I end by saying, "Well, here is for a world where people finally find out that Christ's teachings and God alone will make a happy world to live in. Love, Bill"

One vivid memory of our time in Furth was walking out of the mess hall and finding a group of German civilians all lined up to accept any leftovers that we might be throwing away. It was such a pitiful sight. We could see they were thin and undernourished and in need, some horribly so, especially some of the children. I have included a picture of two of the boys we tried to help. We would give them what we had left over, and many of us made sure we always had something "left over."

*Two half-starved German kids*

An August 10 letter mentions going to Nuremberg to see Bob Hope. But it rained and the show was moved from Soldiers Field, where thousands could have taken part, to the Nuremberg Opera House, which only held about 1,000 altogether. So we did not get to see Bob Hope. In the same letter I write about how we were supposed to guard the POWs. I then go on to tell how we soon found this was not necessary, since the prisoners were very thankful we were giving them a place to sleep and seeing to it that they had plenty of food. The result was that the fellows became very careless. For example, after the prisoners boarded the truck, the guard would also get aboard. How? By handing his rifle to one of the prisoners, and then getting aboard and standing so close to the prisoners that they could have easily overpowered him. Of course this was a reference to our situation at Marktheidenfeld. Our work as MPs in Furth was much different as the next letter shows.

August 12: **"Last night my squad was on guard from 2300-0200 Sunday morning. It was a dark starlit night, and a lot of fellows were wandering around town lost. We got them headed the right way after while. At 2230 we had a big 'raid' to catch all civilians out after curfew. We got about 100, which in a way isn't so many considering how big the city is. We turned them right over to the civilian police."**

In letters dated August 13 and 14, I tell how I am trying to learn to type. Then I mention visiting the old walled city of Nuremberg: **"A moat and high wall surround the place. It is a good square mile or so in area, if not more. . . . Soldiers Field, where Hitler used to hold all his big outings, is quite a place. It isn't nearly as** large as I thought it would be." August 16: "I heard a German presentation of the Nutcracker Suite, and it was good. Then, today I spent most of the afternoon looking over old Nuremberg. It is really marvelous to see how well the Germans can adjust to a situation. I was walking down one street when I noticed a hole at the pavement level. It was about 18 inches square. It probably was an opening to the basement. I looked in and it was a little series of rooms where a German family had set up living quarters. The place above them was a pile of rubble. Just an occasional chimney stuck out of the pile of rubble, bricks, dirt, and blocks of stone. Right in the middle of a 200 or 300 yard circle of this rubble and stuff, twists a street, and in the midst of the road, next to the sidewalk, I found a butcher shop. Inside were neat cutting blocks, shining scales, and what looked to me like a lot of meat. The Germans sure like to keep things clean. . . . The German people don't give us a fraction of the trouble that our own or allied troops do." August 17: "Everything goes much the same around here. MP duty is going along better now that everyone knows his job."

On August 20, I received a letter from Happy (Clark Cavett): He tells how after we left the 99th Division, "the Division split into a thousand pieces," and that he was at Camp Lucky Strike at Le Havre, France, waiting to be shipped home. He is part of a discussion group and says, "I have been arguing with those old fundamentalists every night until they think I am crazy. I don't believe I can stand to go back to America and live among people that are so narrow and one-sided. Too, I am thoroughly disgusted with the average GI's attitude—

cussing, yelling vulgar remarks at women, and their dirty filthy minds. . . . I have met a POW that I captured last December and I have had nothing to do—he does everything for me." Happy and I later lost contact, parted partly because of his very liberal ideas. But I sure agreed with him about the immorality of so many in the service. At first I blamed the Army for this, but then realized that the men had brought their way of life with them into the Army.

On August 20th I write: **"When we first came to Furth all the stores were closed except for one or two, here and there. Well, today it seemed like they were all open."**

August 23: **"Today an English speaking Latvian came to the MP office. He said that all the people look to America to make the world free for all to live as they please. He then explained that all the Europeans were afraid of Russia. He said that living under Stalin was the same as living under Hitler. He said that all of the DP's (Displaced Persons) wanted to go to the U.S. but it seemed very impossible."**

August 24: **"The 75 or over point men are to leave soon."** August 29: **"I'm sending a package home. It contains two of those brush sets I was telling you about and some more film."** (Our MP office was in the front office of a building in which a man had produced women's hair brushes. We had gotten acquainted with the owner and had bought some of his brushes which he assembled as we watched.) **"Our jail is in Nuremberg. I put a couple of guys in it the other day.**

The jail looks just like Sing Sing in the movies. . . . Goering, Ribbontroff, and the rest are in the same place as our guys, only you can't see them because the guards won't let anyone even close to the part they are in." August 30: "We had a little change in the MP routine. At 4 this morning the civilian police woke us up and said that a GI was lying in the street in a pool of blood. Too much whiskey. He had fallen out of the second story window to the pavement below. Being drunk he thought he was going through a door. It looked like he had a broken jaw, sprained right leg and ankle and was suffering badly from shock. The German civilians had picked him up and taken him into the house and fixed him up the best anyone could without being a doctor. The Germans are pretty nice people in most ways it seems."

My parents had sent an article highly critical of Patton's crack-down on the GI's. Since we had been the ones who carried out the crack-down, we could see why he had done what he had. So I wrote to my parents: **"The fellows were speeding through town, riding any number of persons in a vehicle, and many other things. The result was various accidents that ended in at least one person getting killed each day. Since we have come in that has gone down now to where there is only an occasional accident."** In this letter of August 30th I bring out one thing which all of us at that time seemed to agree upon. . . . **"From what I have seen of the average German soldier he isn't an awful lot different from the average American soldier. The SS troops were a bunch of trained gangsters that everyone feared, even the German civilians. I believe that** is true because the DP's are always saying that the German civilian was a good person and that the German soldier and civilian both feared any SS person." (Notice how a distinction was made been a German soldier and the SS troopers. We noticed that this distinction between the two groups of German soldiers was universal.)

September 1: "Yes, we have a large number of tanks in the Nuremberg/Furth area. I wouldn't want to guess how many though. . . . Important places are guarded by men armed with rifles. We guard two munitions factories both I. G. Farben institutions."

The fellows pulled a trick on me around September 1, and got my parents all upset. They talked me into getting my picture taken with a cute teenage German girl. They then had it made up on a postal card and wrote on it, **"Dear Mom, They have girls here in Germany. How am I doing? Love, Red."** It is obviously not my handwriting, and I never signed my name as "Red." The first I knew about it was when my parents asked about it. I have just shown this to my wife. I had completely forgotten about it. But now 50-plus years later my wife sees it and thinks the prank was hilarious. Ah, me!

On September 3, 1945, I went down to a creek that ran by our billets. I met three Germans boys, ages 15, 12 and 8. I had an awful time talking to them since my German was so poor, and they knew no English. Then a 17-year-old boy came up who could speak English. We got to talking and since I found he had been in the Wehrmacht (Regular German Army) I asked him about the SS. I write: **"He said that they** were no good. He then described what would happen to you if you didn't do what they said. It all amounted to a hanging or worse. He said that he had to go into the Army or the German SS would punish his father and mother. It seems that it was true of any resistance that the German people tried to offer to the Germans in power."

On September 4: "**Walking down town today I noticed that Woolworths is getting ready to open. It will be about the last store to open in Furth. Furth at present is a pretty thriving metropolis.**" On the 5th: "**What you said about the way Grandma acted when she read that letter sort of amused me. It seemed to take the same effect on her that it did on me when I was in the hospital. I'd fight the war over every night and get a little sick. I wasn't the only one though. We used to all sit up at night and talk instead of going to bed. For some reason when you get all rested up and start thinking about what you have been through it just makes you sick. Until the war ended in Europe we all sweated it out as we say. I don't think being careful alone has much to do about getting killed or not. It is a good 99% the grace of God. I've been fired on at point blank range, as have others. . . . I saw an all G. I. show last night. . . . It was

*"The cute teenage German Girl"*

excellent. A majority of the actors or participants were professionals that had been drafted."

September 11: "Guess what, I got a package today from you. It contained two cans of candy. So I've just started on it, but it really is good. Everyone is enjoying it a lot. - No, I only use the typewriter when I feel like it and can get it. I mostly serve as an information bureau. There are so many outfits in town that people are trying to find, and everyone is moving so much the MP's have to know the 'whereabouts' of them all. I just tell them where. Otherwise I have a guard squad that patrols Furth."

It was about this time that we had a bad time with some Russians. Displaced persons were being gathered together and sent back home, some therefore to Russia. Some of these people did not want to return to Russia. We really wanted to help them stay put, but could do nothing to help them other than ask the Russian soldiers to leave the people be. Well, they insisted that their DP's come with them back to Russia. But they also did something else that we felt we had a right to stop. At the railroad station they "shot up the place." So we had the Russian in charge come and talk to us. He had wrist watches on, up to his elbow. He was one of the roughest, toughest, meanest looking characters that I have ever met. I told him that he had to get his men to stop shooting up into the air, and stop shooting at any old thing they thought was fun to shoot at. Over and over again he answered, "We are allies, you let us do what we want." We finally had to give up and do all we could to get them back on the trains and out of town.

## MARKTHEIDENFELD AM MAIN
### September 14-September 21

September 14: **"Here I am in the 79th Division which has taken the 99th's place. And I am right back where I started from on May 22nd."** I then tell about our trip by truck from Furth back to Marktheidenfeld, and that we had had a minor accident. On the 15th I noted that all the Werhmacht German soldiers have been **"paroled to the Burgermeisters (Mayors) of the towns around here. They seem to be happy and are helping the farmers around here. The cage is now full of SS only. The old PW'S say that that is where the SS belong. 'The SS are no good', is their remark. It seems to be the general feeling of most Germans."** On the 16th: **"Our old PW'S seem to have the free run of the town. I see them all around."** On the 20th: **"Tonight we walked up to see some Germans that I met while we were here before. One is the owner of a good sized lumber factory and furniture place, Dr. Rinkel. He has many friends here and they seem to have all been educated in England. . . . At church Sunday I heard a little sentence that really is true of Europe, 'Crosses, Crosses, Everywhere, but When Will the Christ of Those Crosses be Preached?' That sure is Europe, Crosses everywhere you turn."**

## DACHAU
### September 22-December 7, 1945

September 22, **"I wonder when they will settle down and put us where we are going to stay a while. . . . We are in Dachau, Germany, the place where the prisoners were starved and then cremated. We are living in a big SS

**barracks on the same ground. Our building is 4 stories high, and easily holds the 1,000 men that are in it. I'm now in D Battery of the 135th AAA Battalion that is quartered in this building. .. The radio just said that 45-60 points won't start home until January 1st. . . . The boys are really sore at the way they aren't going home. It sure is hard for me to see what is fair. I'm alive, so I'm not bitching too hard."** (I had only 55 points.)

My stay at Dachau was very interesting. I sent home a diagram of the camp and also the material about the death of so many prisoners. I tell about going to Munich, which was 17 miles southeast of Dachau, and how the Germans had laid down narrow gauge rails and were running small trains with mine-type cars into the wreckage of the bombed out buildings in order to remove all the debris of the bombings. Since I knew how to type, I volunteered to help the Battery clerk. As I was a Staff Sergeant, some of them felt intimidated, since typing is usually done by corporals and below. But I wanted to learn to type better, so they tolerated me. I talked about a lengthy conversation with Dr. Renkel before I left Marktheidenfeld. A few things he said were of special interest to me. He told of how previously he had had 60 Russian and 40 French prisoners of war working for him. He told how he had them fill out questionnaires so he could figure out where to place them in his factory. He said all of the Russians could read and write, but not all of the French. Some of the French people were not even able to write their names. He also talked about the mistreatment of SS prisoners of war. He told how Patton had come by and had seen the SS Camp in Marktheidenfelt and how Patton had noted how skinny the men were. I then write that Dr. Renkel said, "General Patton inspected this camp and since that day they have received good rations." Later he talked about how he felt Germany should be treated and I write that he said, "We are human, and you must treat us as such. If you don't, you again will have fought for nothing. Germany must never rise again, but it can become democratic and help the rest of the world." Notice that by the use of the word "again" Dr. Renkel refers to the mistreatment of Germany after World War I.

October 6: **"I read today that some of the men in congress are thinking of pulling all the men out of Germany. All I can say is that that would be the biggest mistake that they could make. Every European other than the Russians and English look to the U.S. as their only real friend that means what she says. If other nations moved in there would probably be a lot of trouble and undoubtedly the Russians would soon take over like they have every other place. - You would never feel so funny and filled with wonder at coming here and seeing how these people of Europe all manage to mutually hate each other thoroughly."** (Going out to sea from Bremerhaven, on our way home, I remember the feeling of relief I had on leaving a Europe filled with so much hatred.)

On October 8, I tell of my walk around the little city of Dachau and how beautiful it was. Then on the 10th I write that I had been trying to study subjects of interest and had completed a book on electricity. On the 12th of October I write about the people who wanted to give extra points to the men who had been captured, and that they should be discharged regardless of points, since being a captive had been so terrible. I felt that combat was just as hard as being captured.

On the 14th, I included a news article in my letter home: **"Here is the pay-off. A German band for German civilians wearing our 1st Division patch. I am proud** of that patch and I'll be damned if I want to see Jerries wearing it. I don't know what plausible reason there is for such an asinine trick." (Signed, Pvt. Don Dressing, 26th Infantry, 1st Division)

So many things happened, one wonders what to include in this record. On October 20, I write that I was glad they received the hair brushes I had sent and told how the maker claimed to have sold them all over England and South America, before the war. On the 24th I record that we were having trouble in one prisoner of war camp, and how 30 had escaped. Then, **"Sunday the prisoners stood around the fences and taunted the fellows that were on guard. They thought the fellows wouldn't do anything. Finally the fellows shot into them and killed one and wounded several others. These new prisoners seem to think that they can do as they please. I think that they know better now."**

All of us were given opportunity to go on a vacation in the area. I went on a bus tour with a group of fellow soldiers. We visited many places in Bavaria. We spent a night in a hotel beside the majestic Konigsee, which is near Berscheistgarden, Hitler's retreat; then on to the Ettal, a Monastery in the Bavarian Alps. We stopped at Oberammergau (42 miles southwest of Munich) where the Passion Play is given every 10 years. In the town we visited the home of Anton Lang, the man who had played Christ 3 times and became famous because of the way he acted out his part. We saw the absolutely gorgeous castles of Ludvig, the Mad King of Bavaria. On to Garmish, a winter playground for Germany, and then up to Zugspitz, the highest mountain in Bavaria, going into the snow and all. That night we went to a Bavarian inn and enjoyed a German band dressed in their leather shorts and knee-high socks, as they played polkas, sang, and generally put on a good program. The highlight of the trip for me was actually going up to Hitler's mountain hideout. An immense window fronted the main room of this retreat home. It looked out over a beautiful valley that led into Salzburg, Austria, which could be seen off to the east. It was an awesome place. The marble floor had been all broken up, and everyone took home a piece. I still have a hunk of marble from that floor. In all our trip lasted only 3 days. I realize now that such a tour would cost a thousand dollars today. At the time we paid very little. It was a very memorable experience, savored even today. In a letter dated October 29 I say of the Konigsee: **"I sure would like to see it again one of these days."** In that same letter, **"I sure liked the way the President stood pat with the Atomic Bomb. The Germans I know, and me too, are plenty scared of the Russians, and the Atomic Bomb is a good thing to have."**

On October 30 I wrote home: **"You ask the question, 'What do they say about Russia where you are?' Here is what they say, 'Why don't you fight the Russians, they are doing the same things that the Nazis did.' Then they go on and say, 'How can you say we did wrong and punish us and still let the Russians go on doing as we did. They are worse than the Nazis you know.' The Latvians, Poles, Hungarians, etc., all say the same thing except for a very, very few. They also say, 'I will not go back to my country until I know that the Russians are not ruling my motherland. I still think that my country is the best country, but I think it is best that I stay away until they (Russians) go.' I'll add my little bit by saying that these people all mean what they say, and have good reason to say it. All of them want to go to the U.S. or Canada if they can manage it. I've talked to some D.P.s and they**

**tell tales of what has happened to those that have gone home. They aren't nice stories. But I think this is enough for now."**

About this time members of our congregation in Pasadena informed me that they had relatives, Mr. and Mrs. Wolf, in Munich and asked me to visit them, so they sent me their address. They were very worried about their well-being. I visited the Wolfs and found them in fair health, since Mr. Wolf worked at a bakery. From pictures they showed me, I could see they both had lost weight. But the big problem was I spoke so little German, and they so little English. However, we managed to communicate. They had a teenage relative that spoke English, so as often as possible she was present when I visited, and translated. I had many pleasant visits with them. I brought all kinds of food to them. I also offered them money. They didn't want any, saying it really wasn't worth much. People wanted real things, and therefore people were bartering rather than using money. So I gave them cigarettes, since I did not smoke anyhow. You would think that I had given them gold. What smiles broke forth. With cigarettes you could get just about anything you wished. I also brought them powdered eggs. Mrs. Wolf then fixed some for me. (She always seemed to think she had to feed me something.) I had never liked powdered eggs the way our cooks fixed them. Mrs. Wolf's were excellent. One day they asked what I thought of the frauleins, the German girls. I told them that I had nothing to do with them. They all said, "Bravo," and that seemed to end all thoughts that I might be a "bad boy."

On November 3rd I tell of speaking to a fellow that had looked all over the Russian occupied zone for his parents

*Mr. and Mrs. Wolf in better days. Relatives of members of our congregation in Pasadena, California.*

*Mr. Wolf when I met him.*

and other relatives. He found that they were all dead, killed by the Germans. He also listened to a speech by a Russian that ended with "Viva Stalin, Viva Tito," but no mention of the U.S., etc. He said he asked the man why, especially when all the trucks and vehicles that you could see around the place were American. The man said that he had been given a speech to read, and he read it and nothing more.

On the 11th: **"Germany really is a beautiful country. On the way up the truck driver said the same thing several times. Everything is so tidy, clean, and 'just so' looking that it seems like it must be nature's own paradise. The Germans really seem to be the ones that make it so, though. You will often see a group of farmers cleaning up a forest, patching roads, or doing things to help the look of things. I don't know if they have laws saying that the Germans must keep up everything that borders their property, but nevertheless, they do keep it up."**

On November 19, 1945, I sent home a *Stars and Stripes* paper which in bold headlines proclaimed, FOUR-YEAR TROOPS AND 55-POINTERS TO BE ELIGIBLE FOR DISCHARGE DEC. 1. Then I wrote: **"That's me"** under the 55. In an accompanying letter I conclude by writing: **"I hope that you are saving all my letters, because I put in them just about everything that I want to remember and go over later."** Yet here it is over 50 years later. In that time I have never looked at the 353 letters and 18 post cards Mom saved till now. Surely this is an example of how quickly our interests and priorities change.

On the 22nd I report how a group of us had made up a basketball team and won the league playoffs.

On the 23rd: **"We had a nice Thanksgiving dinner. We had turkey, mashed potatoes, peas, stuffing, pumpkin pie, cake. We were waited on by SS men in their black uniforms, and had the officers orchestra play for us. After dinner they gave out one bottle of liquor per three men."** On the 29th: **"I don't know whether I told you, but a bunch of Polish boys have taken over guarding the camp."**

From December 1, 1945, on, I notice that the emphasis in all my letters is wanting to get home and complaining in one way or another about all the delays in getting us back. So in my December 1st letter: **"We are still waiting around, hoping to be moved out before long. Today the 38 pointers left for another outfit."** Then on the 4th: **"The 135th is going home in the latter part of December with 56-58 points."** Since I could type I got involved in all the paperwork that had to be completed for each man before he could be sent back to the U.S. Step by step we moved closer to the date we would get on board ships and return to the U.S.

## MUNICH, GERMANY
### December 8, 1945-January 12, 1946

*The Basketball team, minus Perkins. L/R—William Martin (We called him CHIEF, since he was Apache Indian), Frank Hartzell, Bill McMurdie, Ramiro Bernal (the star, since he was the best player.)*

December 8, 1945: **"At the present time I am in a castle about 20 miles north of Munich. The trip up here was a cold ordeal. The roads and everything are frozen and it is very cold. The castle has a moat around it and a bridge is the only entrance. . . . A Staff Sergeant has just come in. He is driving to France with 350,000 dollars worth of Radar equipment. He is really angry because he is responsible for the whole works, and an officer is usual responsible for the stuff."** We only stayed at the castle a few days, and then went to a German military camp on the northern outskirts of Munich, about an hour's walk from the Wolfs', and so I visited with them again. I mention talking to them, through the German girl who could speak English, and finding **"that they still don't feel bad except for one thing, and that** is that they lost the war." The outfit to which I was attached ran the P. X. in Munich, and I was given a Jeep with which I took fellows to different type guard duty. It was a very good deal. On the 14th I write: **"Today I watched a group of Germans evacuate a large apartment house to make way for a part of our Occupation Force. It doesn't seem right to throw them out, but that is what is being done."**

December 16: **"I can't seem to stop thinking about a year ago today. We all thought we were done for about this time - 2300. It is funny how clearly I can remember every little thing that happened during the war. I guess that everything that is out of the ordinary is very likely to be impressed on your memory."** (The Battle of the Bulge started on December 16, 1944.) On the 18th I mention taking fellows to guard a warehouse. A chaplain came to our outfit and delivered a "sermon" or speech in which he said we had won "a" war, but not the real war which is the war we all daily fight against the evil in our own lives. My comment was, **"The fellows were absolutely dumbfounded. What he said was too true and we all knew it."** I don't remember or record that he said anything to the effect that only in Christ and what He has done is there victory over sin and death.

December 20: **"The Wolfs were overjoyed with the letter that I brought them from the Maiers. They are hoping that I'll stay around, of course."** December 24: **"It is the night before Christmas and all through the house, can be heard many a soldier getting on his blouse."** So I began the letter written that day. I then go on to mention that I had found the Lutheran Church in Munich, and that Mom and Dad could tell the Maiers that it had not been harmed. The letter of the 27th tells how I spent Christmas Day with the Wolfs and how Mr. Wolf took me to where he worked and showed me around.

## MALMEDY MASSACRE

As the new year of 1946 rolled around, the topic of discussion became the MALMEDY MASSACRE. I notice that in my letter to my parents, dated December 29, 1945, I write: "One event of the Battle of the Bulge was the so-called MASSACRE OF MALMEDY."

What happened, in brief, was this.

Peiper, the commander of the 1st SS Panzer Regiment of tanks and other mobile units, was to race around the 1st Army of about 1 million men to the city of Antwerp on the North Sea. Hitler's plan was to thus surround our 1st Army with his following troops and, using captured supplies, fight off Allied help and take us all prisoners. He believed that the U.S. and England would then sue for peace. (What happened is what we call the Battle of the Bulge, since Hitler's plan failed.)

Hitler's plan failed partly because Peiper's group was stalled on December 16th, the first day of the Battle of the Bulge. The roads were clogged with troops, and the tanks could only use a few roads because of the downed bridges. Also, the 99th and others put up stiff resistance. But on December 17th, Peiper broke out, and one of the first towns he came to was Malmedy. In taking the area he captured 136 men. He soon went on since he was the spearhead of the attack. He left some of his men to keep watch over the prisoners. Suddenly gun fire broke out and cut our men down. So, the so-called MASSACRE AT MALMEDY. And as said, it became a topic of discussion with us in late December 1945. In my letter of the 29th, I mention it and write:

**"Frank Hartzell related the time their Armored Infantry company captured around 150 Germans. They were captured 30 miles inside German lines. It would take at least 10 men and 7 vehicles - combat vehicles remember - to return them. Besides that, they would need an escort to fight any Germans that attack them. The whole idea is out of the question, even if only 5 men had been captured. They therefore lined them up and did their duties as good American soldiers - and future citizens. They killed them all - in cold blood - if you think it should be said that way."**

I then gave them a few other examples of times I had talked to men about doing basically the same thing.

Reading the above you might feel that our men did the wrong thing. You might say, "They could have tied them up!" But if you feel that way try to put yourself in the soldier's place. He is trying to win a battle. It never seems as if you have enough men to do the job. The enemy is fighting back for all he is worth, and the battle is a tough one. Suddenly someone surrenders. But you need to keep on the advance. You don't have men to spare. You have lost men. What do you do? And please notice we are talking about "in the midst of battle." We are not talking about a situation as we had toward the end of the war when Germans were surrendering all over the place and not really fighting back. Of course we took prisoners. We also did it very openly in order to encourage the surrender of others in the area. We had a fellow who spoke flawless German, and he would try to talk the Germans into surrendering, and sometimes they did. Prisoners are taken when it is practical to do so. But sometimes it is not practical. I personally am not so sure that it was right to picture what the Germans did at Malmedy as a massacre, especially when I knew we were doing the same thing under the same circumstances.

I have read two books about the so-called Malmedy Massacre. One is *Massacre at Malmedy* by Charles Whiting, originally written in 1971. He tells about what happened almost as if he were there. He even gives the name of the man who is supposed to have fired the first shot, a Rumanian by the name of Goerg Fleps, who had been drafted into Hitler's army. Then he pictures how other German soldiers joined in cutting down the GIs. And I don't want to say that what happened was not tragic, it was. But having personally been in combat, I can just see someone writing about things we did and wonder if it could not be pictured in much the same way. If we had lost I think it would have. And one wonders—what do such people think war is like anyway? Do they think the enemy soldiers say, "Hey, I am the enemy and I know I should be killed so please kill me?" Let me tell you, they shoot at you and its not nice at all, and you cannot but feel that you have the right to self defense and you shoot back hoping the other guy is the one who dies, not you. I always thought General Patton had it right. He would say to the troops, "Men, I am not asking you to die for your country. I am asking you to make sure the enemy dies for his country."

The other book, entitled *The Malmedy Massacre,* is by John Bauserman. He researched the whole incident in such detail, one wonders how he ever found the time to do what he has done. It includes interviews with both American and German soldiers involved in the incident. He gives the story from both the German side and the American side. His book was published in 1995, written then after the passions of war have somewhat subsided. His presentation is very objective. He points out that the German battle-group commander, Peiper, never gave any order to shoot the 136 or so prisoners, but that suddenly someone did start shooting, but no one has ever figured out who. He then says:

> *Historians here note that Peiper did ascertain. . . that in certain battle conditions prisoners of war (POWs) were to be shot if local conditions of combat warranted it, for example, (1) if POWs could not be guarded, (2) if they were interfering with combat operations, or (3) if they were escaping.* Bauserman also notes: *However, historians also note that Kampfgruppe Peiper* (battle-group leader Peiper) *sent over 600 POWs to the rear during the Eifel Counteroffensive.* (What we called the Battle of the Bulge, the Germans called the Eifel Counteroffensive.) [Underlined are my additions.]

After reading Bauserman's book, I must say that I am saddened to read that after shooting the prisoners as they did, German soldiers from later passing tanks and other vehicles shot into our soldiers lying there dead or wounded. It surely is a reminder that war is a terrible thing. But I also think that it is worthy of note that 54 of the men survived the Massacre, many in spite of being badly wounded. I also think it is interesting to read a letter from a man actually in the fighting at the time. He is also from our 99th Infantry Division. He wrote to Kampfgruppe Peiper after the war as follows:

*I know you faced charges of having your men shoot prisoners of war at Honsfeld, Bullingen and Malmedy. Because we were not molested after a day of severe battle with the best German troops, I have always though you had been accused of something for which you had no control. It is well known that in the heat of battle tempers flare and men will do things they normally would not do. Many situations like this happened with our troops.* (Letter by Lt. Lyle Bouck, as recorded in Major Rusiecki's book, p. 154, see Bibliography.)

War is a terrible thing. It is most sobering. It helps one realize the terrible evil that corrupts us all, and that the only solution is the one provided by God, namely the Good News that Christ died for all, and that through faith in what He has done we have forgiveness of sins, eternal life, and a new nature that helps us do right. But since Christ says that there will be wars and rumors of wars until the end of time, we are reminded that in this life each Christian is fighting a constant battle against evil on many fronts. In my struggle over the years to answer the WHY? of WWII, I must confess that I have come to the conclusion that war is often "idea logical." It was also the false ideas of Hitler that led to the war.

Hitler had come to believe that God had raised him up to bring about a new social order which would bring about at least a great period of peace and prosperity for Germany, if not the world. So his movement, National Socialism. Through government controls he would bring about a perfect social order. And he was highly successful at first, and thus won the hearts of many Germans. But then slowly the people began to realize all was not well, since he believed certain people were the cause of all the evils of society, namely Communists, Jews and anyone who opposed him. So he put the Jews and others into prison. Records of Dachau show that about 15,000 Protestant and Catholic clergy were imprisoned in Dachau, and only half of them got out alive.

But mainly Hitler believed in Socialism, the idea that no one has the right to private property, but all property belongs to the state and should be managed by government for the good of all. Of course what is not admitted is that the person in government who controls the use of a given piece of property essentially becomes the new owner. That they "own it" should be obvious since the government officials often use their power for their own personal gain. And some do notice that while they have no car, the government official has one. While they have no vacation home, the government official has one. While the citizen has little in the way of money, the government officials have plenty.

They also turn their backs on God. The government (read, certain mere human beings) claim all power and wisdom. Man becomes his own God. He decides what is right and wrong.

So behind WWII was surely the evil we all have within us and allowing it to control things, rather than trusting in God and walking in His ways, and fighting against the evil within. Part of the problem was not seeing God's purpose for government: to restrain the natural evil of each of us by protecting life and property; of being the referee while otherwise letting people do what they believe is best. I mention this here since we are almost at the end of my time in the Army. Although I would at first spend two years in college training to be an engineer as I had always planned, I began to think there was something more important that needed doing. Thoughts of life, its meaning and purpose, became foremost. Having seen the ruin of Germany, it seemed such a waste to be an engineer and build things which would last only a while. What was needed most was showing people who God is and finding answers to "life," and thus "build" people who would be good citizens of our nation and of the eternal kingdom of God.

### HOMEWARD BOUND

I saw the New Year in at the Wolfs' home in Munich. Letters more and more talk about when are we going home? January 5: **"Do you know why I won't be home now before March 1st? Because according to General Mac Nair, 600,000 men must be kept in the ETO (European Theater of Operations)."**

Some of us wrote a letter to the editor of a newspaper about the problem. Others took other action. So *Stars and Stripes* reported in a headline:

### "2,000 TROOPS STAGE PROTEST MARCH ON REDEPLOYMENT"

What I did not realize until years later was that the communists in Russia were trying to use us to their own ends. They wanted the soldiers out of Europe so they could take over more of it. They were doing as their official doctrine says to do: note a "social force," that is, a powerful feeling among people. Then organize those people to gain what those people want, but only for the purpose of gaining what you want, political power. After you gain political power then do what you know is "best." This is the way Lenin gained power in Russia. The people wanted land. He promised the people land, and gave it to them at first. But once he was in power, the land was collectivized, and all the other ideas of the Socialists were carried out. But at the time we really wanted to get home and never thought of ourselves as people who were being used by someone to gain their goal.

January 8, 1946: **"Today I am 21 years old. It hardly seems possible. . . . I spent a happy Sunday with the Wolfs and some friends of theirs. We talked, they played different music, and then we talked some more. Their oldest daughter speaks good English so we get along."** January 10: **"We are still here cursing the people who think that we should stay here and occupy Germany while there are others that should be doing it by reason of fairness. . . . The weather has been terrible lately. Great rivers of fog make driving a nerve-wracking job. Fellows have gotten lost for hours trying to get back to camp."**

It was the worst fog I have ever been in. We took the Jeep out just at dusk to pick up some guys. We soon realized that we would never make it. We could not see the oncoming traffic until they were right on top of us, and we also could not really tell where the road was. We drove back and barely made it. We were so worried about the Jeep that we decided to put it into a large garage used for repairing vehicles. I had the fellow that was with me drive the Jeep while I guided him. When we got to the garage, I just pointed out the edge of the building. He drove in. For some reason, after he got out, he walked around in front of the Jeep. He disappeared out of sight, just like that. He had fallen into the grease pit. Neither one of us had seen it, even though the headlights were on. We looked at the placement of the tires, and the tires on the driver's side were only half on the edge of the pit. It was one scary night.

We were still upset about not getting home. So on January 10th a group of 4 of us got permission to go to 3rd Army Headquarters, which was at Bad Tolz, to see the I.G. (Inspector General). This is the group in the Army that you can go to and get any injustice straightened out. I wrote: **"We wanted to know why we weren't getting home. He gave us a pretty good answer."** (It surely is hard to put the best construction on everything, as we want others to do when we do something.)

## WUNSIEDEL, GERMANY
### January 13-February 2, 1946

January 13: **"I'm now in the 283rd Engineers, 'C' Battalion about 20 miles from Czechoslovakia. It took all day to get here from Munich."** I then describe the beauty of the area, how I was involved in typing again, and how the group of men in the group had varied qualifications: a river man (knew how to run boats of all sorts), 100 medics, 100 truck drivers, 5 stenographers, 4 personnel sergeants, rifle experts, electricians, mechanics. My comment: **"It shows you that the Army is one awfully complicated machine. We were all in this unit because of the number of points we had. Then a** problem developed. Too many men were sent to us."

On the 19th I write: "I still remember that mess. Some had to sleep in halls, others in clothes closets." On the 21st: "The siren has just stopped sounding so it must be about 2215. This is the first town in Germany where I have heard the siren used as a warning of the 2230 curfew for civilians. It seems to be a good idea. . . sending the extra men up here has brought about hard feelings and misgivings. By tomorrow we will be down to our proper strength which is 688 men plus 34 officers. The extra 151 men will be sent to the 243rd Engineer Combat Battalion."

I received a letter from the Wolfs, through a friend, Ed Price. Knowing I was going home I had asked him to help the Wolfs as long as he could. They heard I was on the way home and wrote a letter I have just had translated. In it the folks wish me well and thank me for all the efforts I had made in their behalf.

January 23: "Another day closer, but exactly to what I don't know."

January 26: "All our extra equipment has been loaded on the train that is here in Wunsiedel."

January 28: "As far as we know we will move to Bremerhaven some time soon."

January 29: "We are going to start for Bremerhaven on the 30th if nothing bad happens."

## BREMERHAVEN, GERMANY
### February 3 - February 16, 1946

February 3: "We are now at the Port of Bremerhaven. ... We are based at a German Airport. We are in a hanger that has been rebuilt into a barracks. The Engineers built a second floor above the main floor. They did a good job. Each floor holds about 1,000 men. The place has showers and everything."

February 5: "The weather here is really something to complain about. If it isn't raining the wind is blowing so hard that it is a problem to walk down the road. The wind blows in strong gusts that leave you in almost any position when it suddenly stops. This morning it was the worst that it has been. It was blowing so hard that I was stopped dead, and then when I was going the way the wind was blowing I started to run. It was all very perturbing. ... You might be interested in the fact that Negroes and Whites are mixed here. We eat together and have the same Red Cross and Theaters."

February 6: "If all goes well we will be on board and on our way about the 16th."

Sure enough, we got off on February 16. While we waited some of us worked at getting all the records up to date and paying the men money owed them. Other than that we spent most of our time playing cards, going to the Red Cross to enjoy donuts and coffee and conversation, and generally just taking it easy and waiting. The only unique thing I remember was that we had to turn in all extra clothing and shoes. We could only take home one pair of combat boots. I had two pair, and really wanted to keep both. I made a comment along that line, and one of the fellows said, "Don't worry." I had no idea what he meant. The next day he presented me with one of the nicest pair of slippers I have ever owned. At first I did not realize what he had done. He had cut down the boots to make the slippers. It was a masterful job, but I still don't think that it was the right thing for him to have done. When I told him so, he just laughed at me. I don't remember his name, but since we had plenty of time to talk, we talked about our lives before getting into the service. He had been a professional strike breaker. I asked what that meant. He explained that it meant that people paid him to break up a strike in any way he could. This included roughing people up and threatening people. I can't say as I liked to hear what he had to say.

## AT SEA
### February 16-February 25, 1946

We went home on the *USS Waterbury Victory,* a cargo ship converted into a troop ship. I find that I have a copy of the ship's newspaper from this trip home. It tells us that our trip would be 4,000 miles and that we were going 18.32 mph. There was a 21-man engine crew. At printing time we were 30 miles north of Carvo Island, the northernmost island of the Azores. It explained that we would soon hit the Gulf Stream, which actually was a 5,000 mile long warm stream of water, 50 miles wide as it passed Florida, 86 degrees in temperature, and traveling at 4 mph. It would be 75 degrees in temperature by the time it reached England and was the cause of that country's temperate climate.

I remember little about the trip except for two things. First was the gambling. They had paid the fellows before we got on board with the idea that when we got to Camp Kilmer, New Jersey, we would be processed quickly, and should have the money ahead of time. With all the money though, we turned into a gambling den. Two or three men ended up with most of the money, thousands of dollars. It was the talk of the ship. People wondered if the fellows would get off the ship alive. I wondered myself. (They did.) The other thing was the terrible storm. We all got sick. It was so bad they could not serve food for a day or two. They just gave us apples and oranges. Then the ship got into waves that looked to me to be 40 or 50 feet high. The ship would climb up the side of the wave. Then it would go over the top and come to a point where the props were out of the water and the whole ship would shake as the propellers turned in the air. Then down the sloping wave we would go, and it seemed like we were going right down to the bottom of the ocean. We would plow into the next wave and as the ship leveled off, the water would go over the tops of not only the 1st but also the 2nd deck. A special watch was posted at the doors of these two decks so no one would go out. We really did not enjoy this part of the trip.

But then we came into New York harbor. We were all on deck as we went by "The Lady," the Statue of Liberty. There was not a dry eye aboard. It was the most beautiful sight I had ever seen. So often we had thought we would never get back home. While I was in Germany, the U.S. had seemed so far away. Then there had been the constant fear and terrors of the war. "The Lady" really was glorious to see for what it now meant. We were home. We got off to the playing of a band and the greetings of some officials. We were trucked to Camp Kilmer, New Jersey, for processing. I can still remember walking right up to a phone booth and calling up my parents at Sycamore 65137, as if I had not been gone but a few days. I was amazed that I remembered the number, and still do.

It seemed like no time before we were taken to the airport and boarded a DC-4. In a notebook I record that we took off from La Guardia Field at 2030 EST and landed at Tulsa at 0330 EST. After getting 1,700 gallons of fuel, we took off at 0315 CST and landed in Long Beach at 1130 CST. We left Long Beach at 0905 PST and landed at Miles Field at 1130 PST. I especially remember going over the mountains in Southern California and having the airplane caught in an updraft. Guys were walking up the aisle and suddenly could not walk. Then we went over the mountains and we were caught in a down draft, and the fellows who were up walking shot up the aisles. A few hurt themselves, hitting the ceiling and seats. We landed in Long Beach, but stayed only a short while as noted, and then went on to the airport near Sacramento. From the airport outside Sacramento we went by bus to Camp Beal for final processing. They tried to talk us into staying in the Army. They also wanted us to keep our life insurance. They issued us all the medals to which we were entitled and gave us our official discharge papers. I don't know of anyone who re-enlisted. I wish I had kept my life insurance, but for some reason I did not want to have anything to do with the Army any more. That turned out to be a big mistake, since the insurance was good and paid dividends, something I had not even realized it could do.

And then home. I tried to hitchhike, being in such a hurry. But, no rides were offered, so I caught a bus, and finally made it to Pasadena. It was really good to get home and be with the family once again. There is really no way to describe it other than to say that I am very thankful to God that I not only made it through the war, but especially that I was brought up in a family where God and His Word were always first, and we were once more together again.

## EPILOGUE

It is now January in the year 2000, and I have just turned 75, an age to which I really never thought I would reach. Almost 50 years in the Gospel ministry has also brought me to realize that World War II was not just the result of Hitler's desire for revenge because of the bad treatment Germany got after World War I, nor just the result of false ideology. In the final analysis war is a terrible judgment of God against a society. If we think God had nothing to do with our victory, we should consider what would have happened if the Atomic Bomb had been in the hands of Hitler on December 16, 1944, the first day of the Battle of the Bulge.

But God blessed our nation with victory in World War II. And events since do give me a sense of having taken a part in something that has become a blessing to many people. A fellow 99th Division soldier, now Dr. Lyle J. Bouck, expresses it this way in his foreword to Major Stephen M. Rusiecki's book, *THE KEY TO THE BATTLE OF THE BULGE: The Battle for Losheimergraben.* Bouck there writes:

> In 1991, a group of us returned to visit our old battlefield. I walked up the hill near Lanzerath, entered the remains of my old crumbling foxhole, and looked out over the field to the front. I closed my eyes and in a flash relived December 16, 1944. For the first time, I realized a part of me was still in that hole. Goose bumps rose on my skin and chilled me. I walked down the hill to join others in the group. We

then dedicated a beautiful monument that honored the 99th Infantry Division. We found the compassion and expressions of gratitude offered by the proud and loving people of rural Belgium, especially the children, exhilarating and heart warming. This testimony allowed us to believe that our hardships and sacrifices of five decades ago were worth the effort.

There is another thing that has led me to believe that we did accomplish something positive and helpful in service to our country and the world. It is the letter of appreciation received by our commanding general, Major General Lauer, on September 17, 1945, just before the deactivation of our 99th Infantry Division. It reads as follows:

HEADQUARTERS
ARMY GROUND FORCES
OFFICE OF THE COMMANDING GENERAL
Army War College
Washington

17 September 1945

SUBJECT: Letter of Appreciation

TO: Commanding General, 99th Infantry Division

Colorful and courageous in action, the officers and men of the 99th Infantry Division made a magnificent contribution to the glorious victory over a swaggering Nazi enemy sworn to destroy our cherished American way of life. A grateful Nation will always remember the heroism and self-sacrifice of these men of the 99th Division, and acknowledge the hardship and suffering they endured to accomplish their important military missions.

From the time the untried troops of the Checkerboard Division moved out in a driving snowstorm on 13 December 1944 to seize their first objective on the outer fringes of the Siegfried Line until the collapse of Nazidom nearly five months later, they fought with tenacity and skill.

These remarkable fighting men of the 99th, in combat only four days and outnumbered five to one when von Rundstedt's fanatical forces struck the Division's 20-mile front, inflicting casualties in the ratio of eighteen to one to win high acclaim for gallantry in the Battle of the Ardennes. This same zeal and ability to fight against great odds carried the 99th through the Rhine River Campaign, the fighting for the Remagen Bridgehead, into the Ruhr Pocket and finally into the Danube River Drive.

It is noteworthy that the Checkerboard Division captured 42,283 prisoners in the Ruhr Pocket alone, that it became the first Infantry division of the First Army to reach the Rhine, and that it was the first complete Infantry division to cross the historic river.

The pattern for the 99th Division's fame and fighting ability was set soon after its activation, 15 November 1942, at Camp Van Dom, Mississippi. Initial training was followed by maneuvers in Louisiana and further training at Camp Maxey, Texas, before the Division sailed for England, 29 September 1944. First division to land at Le Havre, France, during World War II, the 99th was committed to the lines on 9 November 1944.

Now, upon the inactivation of the 99th Infantry Division, it is my deep privilege to join all America in commending you, and your officers and men for their gallant accomplishments on the field of battle. Such devotion to duty will never be forgotten.

Jacob L. Devers
General, USA
Commanding

Having now written these memoirs, I realize more than ever before that I had the awesome, unsought-after experience, of fighting as an Infantrymen in World War II, and surviving to write about it. I find my thoughts about my experiences very well expressed by Joe Synder, in his book *Para(graph) Trooper for MacArthur,* (Leathers Publishing, 4500 College Blvd, Leawood, Kansas 66211, pp. 99-100). I have altered his words slightly since he served in the Pacific, while I served in Europe.

"I took part in several great waves of battle which washed over the open fields and dense forests of Belgium and Germany, embracing in its fury platoons, companies, regiments, divisions, and armies of brave men who pressed forward into battle because they believed what American has is worth fighting for. Many fell on the meadows and in the forests because of an allegiance not just to a flag but because of an ideal of human dignity that alone was worth the walk into enemy fire.

"Great men, with futures and dreams, men of promise, the sturdy oaks of America as well as the thorny bushes, were swept by the fury of war into a soldier's grave alone in a strange and faraway land."

Among them were two friends I can never forget because of their bravery and devotion to America, and what is good and right about our country—PFC Robert Ison and First Lieutenant Charles Gullette Jr. A feeling of awesome sorrow for the tragedy of war and the loss of so many good men will always remain with me. But with it is also the wonderful confidence that through faith in the Risen Christ there is victory and the glory of the world to come, where war is no more. It is also my prayer that all my fellow citizens of America return to the principles upon which our country was founded and which has made our country great, lest these men have died in vain. It is my hope that Christians will be encouraged in their faith because of what I have written, while those who are not Christians might be encouraged to examine what Christ really taught.

**TO GOD ALONE ALL GLORY**

## HONOR ROLL

*"DAUNTLESS" - A History of the 99th Infantry Division* by William C. C. Cavanagh, published by Taylor Publishing Company of Dallas, Texas, includes within its pages an HONOR ROLL of the 1,181 members of the 99th Infantry Division who are known to have died in Europe. The information given for each man includes the following: name, service number, home state, rank, cause of death, place of first interment, and place of final interment. The bodies of 58% were repatriated to the United States from July of 1947 to December of 1951.

What I have done below is set forth what I might call my personal HONOR ROLL. They are the men I knew personally, who died beside me on the field of battle, and men I have written about in the preceding pages.

KIA (killed in action) is followed by the date killed. (The date might be a day or two off.) What is listed below is the man's name, service number, rank, cause of death and date, and place of final interment as I found them listed in *"DAUNTLESS."* Also, recall that all were members of "A" Company, 394th Infantry Regiment, of the 99th Infantry Division. NCm means National Cemetery. HENRI CHAPELLE refers to the place where the men are buried who were not returned to the U.S.

## Honor Roll (Continued)

* * * * * * * *

**CONRATH, Leon**  A0-1296176   IN   1LT   KIA   03 Mar 45
PENN

**DORNER, George**  W35536179   OH SGT   KIA   18 Dec 44
OHIO

**GULLETTE, Charles Jr.**  RO-1314008   -   1 LT   KIA
17 Mar 45   ARK,   Fort Smith NCm

**HAEFNER, Albert**  W37617905   MO   PFC   KIA   18 Dec 44
Belgium, HENRI CHAPELLE, D-10-31

**HENRY, Sherwood**  D20462854 MS   PFC   KIA   17 Mar 45
MISS

**ISON, Robert**   L35077308   WV   PFC   KIA   18 Dec 44
W.VIR

*HEROES ARE THE PEOPLE WHO DO WHAT HAS TO BE DONE, WHEN IT NEEDS TO BE DONE, REGARDLESS OF THE CONSEQUENCES.*
(Author unknown)

## SOURCES CONSULTED

**BOOKS**

Bauserman, John M. — *The Malmedy Massacre.* Shippensburg, Pennsylvania: White Mane Publishing Co., 1995.

Cavanagh, William C. C. — *"DAUNTLESS" - A History of the 99th Infantry Division.* Dallas, Texas: Taylor Publishing Co., 1994.

Lauer, Walter E. — *Battle Babies, The Story of the 99th Infantry Division in World War II.* Nashville, Tennessee: The Battery Press, 1950.

Rusiecki, Stephen M. — *The Key to the Bulge, the Battle for Losheimergraben.* Westport, Connecticut: Praeger Publishing, 1996.

Snyder, Joe — *Para(graph) Trooper for MacArthur.* Leawood, Kansas: Leathers Publishing, 1997.

Shirer, William 1. — *The Rise and Fall of the Third Reich.* New York: Simon and Schuster, 1960.

*The Collapse of the Third*

| Whiting, Charles | *Republic: An Inquiry into the Fall of France in 1940.* New York: Simon and Schuster, 1969. |
|---|---|
| | *Massacre at Malmedy.* London: Leo Cooper Publishing, 1971. |

## PAMPHLETS

| Haseltin, James L | "The Combat History of the 394th Infantry Regiment." 394th Infantry Special Services, 1945 |
|---|---|
| Camp Maxey | "A Camera Trip through Camp Maxey." Public Relations Office. Brooklyn, New York: The Ullman Co. 1944. |

## PERSONAL INTERVIEWS
### of men in the 99th Inf. Division

| Byers, Richard H. | C Battery—371st Field Artillery, by phone and mail |
|---|---|
| Dudley, George W. | A Company—394th Infantry Regiment, by phone |
| Eubanks, Charles | A Company—394th Infantry Regiment, by phone |
| Hancock, Stanley | A Company—394th Infantry Regiment, by phone |
| Meehan, Dick | A Company—394th Infantry Regiment, by phone |

## LETTERS, ETC

353 letters and 18 postal cards kept for me by my parents. (A number of these letters and cards were mailed to friends and neighbors who then gave them to my parents.)

The story of my war experiences written at Furth, Germany, August 2-September 14, 1945

My memories of these events that I have carried with me all these years.

# APPENDIX 1

Section 0-1 A.S.T.P., University of Arkansas, Fayetteville

| NAME | ADDRESS |
|---|---|
| Myron Bieber | 713 W. Indiana Ave., So. Bend, IN |
| Erich E. Moreno | 21231 N. Loma Linda Dr., Bel Air, CA |
| Don M. Cabe | Otto, NC |
| Gerald L. McNess | 5380 Linden, Long Beach, CA |
| Herbert E. Babb | 75 Adair Ave. S.E., Atlanta, GA |
| Donald A. Kilpatrick | 270 Church St., Milan, MI |
| Lafe R. Edmonds | 1047 So. 13th E., Salt Lake City, UT |
| Grant E. Anderson | 783 E. 2nd Ave., Prichard, AL |
| Bob D. Boyd | 417 South Olive, Shattuck, OK |
| Clark Bradford Cavett | 417 E. Main St., Morristown, TN |
| Robert F. Bowman | 1301 E. Las Tunas Dr., San Gabriel, CA |
| Alister C. Miller | 3600 Haynie Ave., Dallas, TX |
| Michael E. Michello | 1231 E. 81st St., Cleveland, OH |
| Robert L. Baughman | Skelly Service Station, Pittsfield, IL |
| Dale Miller | Box 694 River Street, Enterprise, OR |
| Edmund J. Arsenault | Box 411, Mexico, ME |
| Charles L. Prentiss | 303 E. 5th Street, Bristow, OK |
| Robert L. Benkman | 1104 Washington Ave. E., Albia, IA |
| Edward Z. Borkowski | 61 Walnut St., New Haven, CN |
| Bill McMurdie | 1954 Brigden Rd., Pasadena, CA |

## APPENDIX 2

(This letter is included so that you may see the emblems of the 99th Division and the 394th Infantry Regiment, representing the junction of the Allegheny and Monongahela Rivers forming the Ohio River at Pittsburgh—originally the 99th being the Pennsylvania Division)

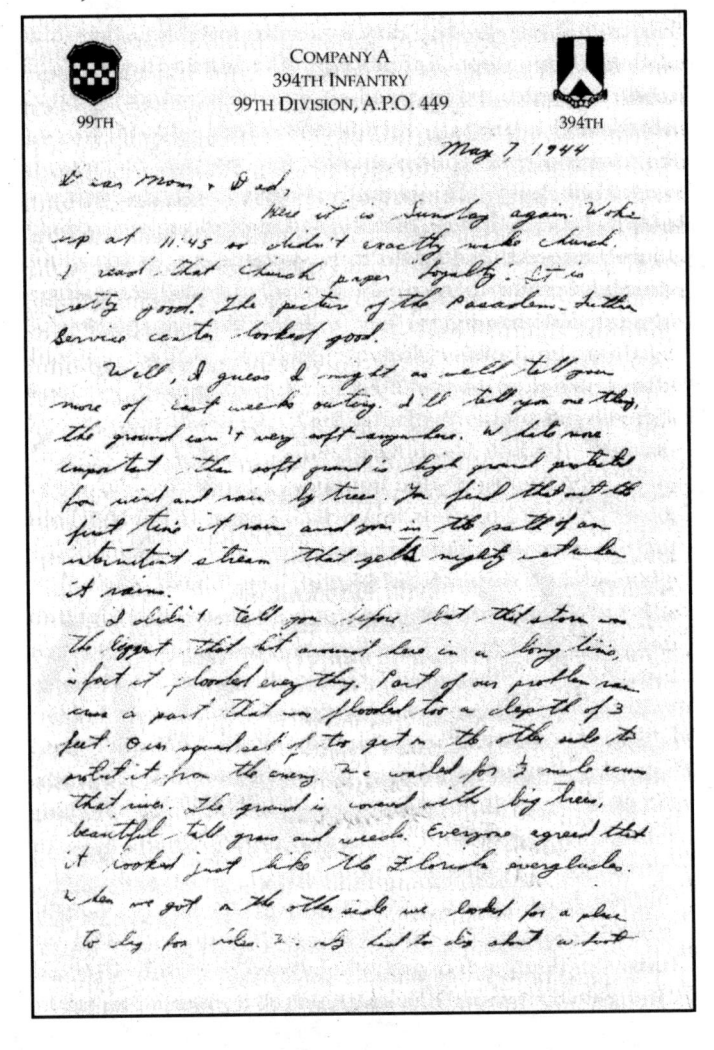

COMPANY A
394TH INFANTRY
99TH DIVISION, A.P.O. 449

99TH            394TH

*May 7, 1944*

*Dear Mom & Dad,*

*Here it is Sunday again. Woke up at 11:45 so didn't exactly make church. I read that church paper "Loyalty". It is pretty good. The picture of the Pasadena Lutheran Service Center looked good.*

*Well, I guess I might as well tell you more of last week's outing. I'll tell you one thing, the ground isn't very soft anywhere. What's more important — the soft ground is high ground suitable for wind and rain by trees. You find that out the first time it rains and you're in the path of an intermittent stream that gets mighty wet when it rains.*

*I didn't tell you before, but that storm was the biggest that hit around here in a long time, in fact it flooded everything. Part of our problem was a part that was flooded too — a depth of 3 feet. Our squad set off to get on the other side to outlet it from the enemy. We waded for ½ mile up that river. The ground is covered with big trees, beautiful tall grass and weeds. Everyone agreed that it looked just like the Florida everglades. When we got on the other side we looked for a place to lay for idea. 2. My had to dig about a foot*

# CONDITIONS IN WHICH THE BATTLE OF THE BULGE WAS FOUGHT
## December 16, 1944 - February 1, 1945

*Note the communications wires at the left, a sign you were not at the front.*

*Note that there are now only two wires. You are much closer to the front.*

*Now you are at the front, expecting action at any moment.*

*Just Me*
*Rest Area in Castle, St, Pierre, Belgium*

*Fellow soldier and me*